FAITH AND ITS CRITICS

Faith and Its Critics

A Conversation

DAVID FERGUSSON

OXFORD

UNIVERSITY PRESS

OXFORD
UNIVERSITY PRESS

Great Clarendon Street, Oxford OX2 6DP

Oxford University Press is a department of the University of Oxford.
It furthers the University's objective of excellence in research, scholarship,
and education by publishing worldwide in

Oxford New York

Auckland Cape Town Dar es Salaam Hong Kong Karachi
Kuala Lumpur Madrid Melbourne Mexico City Nairobi
New Delhi Shanghai Taipei Toronto

With offices in

Argentina Austria Brazil Chile Czech Republic France Greece
Guatemala Hungary Italy Japan Poland Portugal Singapore
South Korea Switzerland Thailand Turkey Ukraine Vietnam

Oxford is a registered trade mark of Oxford University Press
in the UK and in certain other countries

Published in the United States
by Oxford University Press Inc., New York

British Library Cataloguing in Publication Data

Data available

Library of Congress Cataloging in Publication Data

Fergusson, David. Faith and its critics: a conversation / David Fergusson.
p. cm.
Comprises the Gifford lectures delivered in Apr. 2008 at the University of Glasgow.
Includes bibliographical references (p.).
ISBN 978-0-19-956938-0
1. Christianity and atheism.   2. Faith.   3. Apologetics   I. Title.
BR128.A8F47   2009
261.2′1—dc22   2009011167

Typeset by SPI Publisher Services, Pondicherry, India
Printed in Great Britain
on acid-free paper by
CPI Antony Rowe, Chippenham, Wiltshire

ISBN 978-0-19-956938-0

3 5 7 9 10 8 6 4 2

PREFACE

This book comprises the Gifford Lectures delivered at the University of Glasgow in April 2008. I am grateful to the Vice-Chancellor, Sir Muir Russell, for his invitation, and also to the members of the Gifford Committee for their generous hospitality, in particular Professor David Jasper.

The occasion of these lectures provided a welcome opportunity to return to my home city and the *alma mater* where I first studied philosophy more than thirty years ago. I am grateful for the many friends, family, colleagues, and former teachers who attended the six lectures and participated so constructively in discussions each evening, many of them proving thereby that Glasgow and Edinburgh are not so very far apart.

In preparing and writing up the material, I have had to draw upon the expertise of colleagues in a wide variety of fields. For comments, suggestions, and corrections, thanks are owed (in no particular order) to Robert Segal, Steve Sutcliffe, Ian Hazlett, David Clough, Lisa Jane Goddard, Mona Siddiqui, Jeremy Begbie, Gordon Graham, Wilson Poon, Michael Fuller, Perry Schmidt-Leukel, Neil Spurway, Sandy Stewart, Alexander Broadie, Graeme Auld, Hans Barstad, George Newlands, Paul Heelas, Iain Torrance, Larry Hurtado and Christian Lange. I am especially indebted to my former colleague Michael Partridge for reading and commenting at some length on the typescript of the lectures. Our conversations enabled me to gain much greater clarity on many points, though the flaws remain entirely my own. I am grateful also for the assistance of Sean Adams in the preparation of the index.

CONTENTS

INTRODUCTION

THE 'new atheism' is a term coined recently to describe a wave of writings that offer a full-frontal attack on the intellectual claims and moral effects of religion. Associated primarily with Richard Dawkins, it also characterizes the work of other intellectuals who share much of his hostility towards religion. Despite the tendency in some theological circles to dismiss this literature rather scornfully, I consider it worth engaging for several reasons. At the very least, it is incumbent upon theologians of whatever stripe to offer a response to the arguments, criticisms, and dismissal of some of their central claims. The New Testament, which contains a number of references to the philosophy of the ancient world, enjoins its readers to give an account of the hope that is within them.[1] At the same time, the work of the new atheists is intensely interesting; the range of questions and subjects raised are of concern to every person. These can generate a heated discussion in any pub or senior common room. Every human being ought to have an understanding, however implicit, of the nature of the world in which we live, the significance of our lives, and our deepest convictions. To evade this is simply to miss the significance of these questions and the commitments that will inevitably be reflected in the responses we offer.

We live in an age when for many of us there are competing options and different ways of living. Charles Taylor sees this

as one of the most significant differences from the world of
pre-modernity. Belief in God is no longer a default position in
our society. It has become an 'embattled option' that is taken
amidst doubt, criticism, challenge, and the sometimes easier
alternatives of unbelief.[2] One cannot ignore those beliefs that
are different to one's own—we need to gain some appreciation
of what these are like and how they look from the inside, as it
were. In doing so, one might have an enhanced sense of one's
own faith and why it is that one sticks with it. Perhaps the most
important reason for a theological study of atheism is that it
may have something salutary to teach those of us who remain
committed to faith. Of course, this is far removed from the
intention of the new atheists, who advocate the abandonment
of religion rather than its renovation. No quarter is given and
no compromise is sought. Yet the consideration of the most
powerful challenges that can be levelled against religion may
itself enable a clearer and more chastened perception of what it
is one believes and to which one is committed. Jonathan Sacks
has spoken in this context of the ways in which atheists can
save the faithful from believing too much. There are times
and places where silence and scepticism serve us better than
the passionate certainties that may later appear misplaced and
even harmful. At least, this can sometimes happen. The history
of Christian theology reveals that the tradition developed and
was shaped decisively by encounter with opponents and revisionists. Much of what we intuitively believe is the product of
history and patterns of interpretation that have evolved over
many centuries. This process is ongoing. So in what follows
I aim to pursue a more patient and constructive conversation
with the new atheism in the hope that there are possibilities
for occasional alliances and recognition of mutual insights. In
this respect, it will heed Bernard Crick's plea for a coalition
of humanists and believers who can together find ways of
working for common goals even amidst significant intellectual
disagreement.

How new is the new atheism? The present movement probably comes closer to the combative work of Bertrand Russell than to other modes of sceptical thought, particularly the more wistful agnosticism that we find in the late Victorian and Edwardian periods. Hostility to the intellectual claims of religion, the attack on its pathological effects, and the conviction that people can live better without it are all features of several recent high-profile studies. But what is now missing is the elegiac tone. God's funeral, to use Thomas Hardy's phrase, is long since passed. There is no need for mourning. The text of the new atheism might be Psalm 30:5. 'Weeping may linger for the night, but joy comes in the morning.' There is indeed a good deal of confidence that atheism can provide a more wholesome, morally alert, and psychologically liberating way to live. One recent attempt at a psychological profiling of atheists concludes that the typical atheist is male, tolerant, law-abiding, well-educated, and less authoritarian than many of his contemporaries. Atheists, we are assured, make good neighbours.[3]

To a large extent, we are dealing with an English-language movement, although we can find other European thinkers expressing similar sentiments. Today's leading exponents of atheism are: Richard Dawkins, an Oxford scientist; Daniel Dennett, an American philosopher; Sam Harris and Christopher Hitchens, both writers based in the USA (although Hitchens is English); Anthony Grayling, a London philosopher; and Michel Onfray, a French philosopher. These leading figures are all men, a fact that has not gone unnoticed. In her study of the movement, Tina Beattie complains that we are witnessing today a testosterone-charged fight. 'There is something a little comic, if not a little wearisome, about this perennial stag-fight between men of Big Ideas, with male theologians rushing to defend the same pitch that they have fought over for centuries, which is now being colonised by men of Science, rather than men of God.'[4] On the other hand, Beattie herself proves capable of throwing a few good punches.

Much of the debate has been conducted through the internet on websites and blogs. This has resulted in a high level of public participation, although one may wonder whether the phenomenon of blogging tends to encourage extremist sound bites as opposed to more patient deliberation. On the fringes of the movement, there are a significant number of journalists, novelists, and popular thinkers who act as their cheerleaders. Consider Muriel Gray's sycophantic introduction of Richard Dawkins at the 2007 Edinburgh Book Festival. After introducing him as one of the world's top intellectuals, she then declares that he has not merely started a debate but actually closed it. So powerful is his case that the argument is effectively over. There is little more to be said about religion after being confronted by all this 'fantastic evidence'.[5]

The movement also has the support of leading literary figures, including Martin Amis and Ian McEwan. It has been suggested that Henry Perowne, the central character in McEwan's acclaimed novel *Saturday*, resembles an ideal type of new atheist.[6] He is not passionate about atheism or scornful of religion, but he is someone who lives well without any sense whatsoever of the need for faith. A neurosurgeon working in London, Perowne leads a fulfilled professional and personal life. Yet he is perplexed by the political events around him following 9/11 and the war on Iraq. Religion has now become a menacing force on the horizons of his consciousness. In the closing phase of the novel, he looks out from the bedroom window of his London house and contemplates how its original owner a hundred years earlier would have had little comprehension of what awaited the world in the century ahead. So too, the twenty-first century has suddenly become an enigma with the gathering of strange and alien forces that have reached his doorstep.

A hundred years ago, a middle-aged doctor standing at this window in his silk dressing gown...might have pondered the new century's future. February 1903. You might envy this Edwardian gent all he didn't yet know. If he had young boys, he could lose them within a dozen years, at the Somme. And what was their body count, Hitler, Stalin, Mao? Fifty million, a hundred? If you described the hell that lay ahead, if you warned him, the good doctor...would not believe you....Here they are again, totalitarians in different form, still scattered and weak, but growing, and angry, and thirsty for another mass killing.[7]

This recent wave of writings has emerged in the aftermath of the events of 9/11. A world in which religious convictions appear resurgent and dangerous seems different from that inhabited by secularized intellectuals a generation ago. Then religion could be allowed to wither on the vine. The secularization of western society led many to believe that, under the conditions of modernity, religion would gradually disappear as a socially significant phenomenon. It would be reduced at most to a private life-style choice that was both quaint and harmless. Now, however, we are confronted with significant adjustments to the secularization thesis. Fears have been expressed about the emergence of a new Islamic Europe— *Eurabia*. As a result of patterns of immigration, the capacity of Muslim populations with their high fertility rates to outbreed everyone else, and the misguided policy of multiculturalism, Europe, it is argued, soon will unwittingly have a new religious identity. This thesis is further encouraged by the siren call of some American commentators who argue that secular Europe has lost its moral and spiritual direction and is now ready to be conquered. These stark claims have all been patiently refuted and countered by Philip Jenkins in his recent book *God's Continent*, but they persist in the media and are widely circulated.[8]

The dramatic resurgence of religion is even conceded by a recent issue of the *Economist*. Having proclaimed the death of God at the turn of the millennium, the *Economist* now concedes that this was a mistaken diagnosis. Its leader writes, 'God is definitely not dead, but He now comes in many more varieties.'[9] In global terms, religion remains a potent socio-political force. The sociologist Peter Berger in his study of de-secularization describes our world today as being 'furiously religious'.[10] Having abandoned his earlier espousal of the secularization thesis, Berger claims provocatively that what is required is sociological study of the exceptions, for example Swedes and New England college professors.

In its classical form, the secularization thesis was indebted to two of the founding fathers of sociology—Max Weber and Emile Durkheim. The theory of rationality proposed by Weber implied the disenchantment of the world and with it the steady and irreversible decline of religious belief. Having lost its plausibility structure as a result of the encounter with modern science, medicine, and politics, religious faith was no longer sustainable. For Durkheim, the differentiation of functions in a modern society implied that much of what had previously been controlled by the churches was now assumed by professional organizations, secular institutions, and the political state. Following this loss of influence, it was assumed that the activities of faith communities would inevitably decline in terms of their public significance. With this shift in both belief and action, the secularization of modern society has been a widely held axiom of scholars for over a century. Around 73 percent of the world's population now adheres to one of the four global religions—this figure represents a sharp increase from figures earlier in the twentieth century.[11] The counter-example of the USA, the world's wealthiest nation, is perplexing for the classical secularization thesis. This can be dealt with in either of two ways. It may be that America is an exception, requiring particular explanation for the salience of religion there. One might also seek to show that there are some symptoms of religious decline even there. Alternatively, a case can be made to demonstrate that, from a global perspective, Europe is the exception rather than the rule. The resurgence of faith in much of the southern hemisphere and in Asia suggests at the very least that the secularization thesis requires to be significantly qualified. China and India, the world's two most populous countries, do not immediately strike one as travelling on a road to secularization in the slipstream of economic modernization. At the same time, even the most rapidly secularized societies of western Europe may be witnessing not so much the decline of religious activity and belief as its displacement into alternative expressions. Grace Davie's thesis about 'believing without belonging' suggests that human lives continue to be enchanted in significant ways alongside the decline in adherence to traditional institutions. The current interest in 'spirituality' may be symptomatic of this, although some rigorous questioning is required of much of its rhetoric.[12]

Much of today's new atheism is frustrated by the sociological evidence. Religion is resurgent, thus disconfirming much of the Durkheimian thesis. At the same time, the Weberian account of rationality and disenchantment seems intuitively right. Religious faith still lacks plausibility for many intellectuals, thus rendering secularization the only rational outcome. Still in the grip of Weberian assumptions, much modern atheism is therefore not merely dismissive of religion but angry and frustrated by its re-emergence as a powerful social force. This is particularly evident in two ways. First, the American context, with the ongoing wars over the teaching of creation science and intelligent design theory in public schools, remains at the forefront of contemporary debate. Much of the hostility heaped on religion is directed at the perceived obscurantism of evangelical Christianity and its particular disbelief in Darwinian evolution. A second feature of the recent debate concerns what is called 'Islamism', a militant and deviant brand of Islam that advocates violent opposition to the hegemony of western, democratic capitalism. This is sometimes traced to developments from the 1970s onwards, although it is likely that a much longer historical explanation is required for the various dispositions of Islam, particularly in the middle east, towards western culture. For example, the frustration caused by the hegemony of the west has precipitated reform movements in Islam since at least the eighteenth century. Furthermore, the colonial era is perceived by many Muslims to have ideological links with the crusades of the middle ages.[13]

The relationship between theology and sociology is here quite complex. Neither belief nor unbelief requires to be closely annexed to a particular reading of the secularization thesis. One might readily accept it as an explanation of the decline in religious belief and activity in the modern world without assuming that this renders religion untrue or lacking in value. Truth claims, after all, are not settled by counting heads or finding out who is in charge. Conversely, one might recognize that much of the older secularization theory was just too simplistic to deal adequately with the phenomena. At the same time, a sceptic might even claim that human beings are universally disposed to be religious, whether genetically or otherwise, without thereby committing to the validity or ineluctability of faith. In this way, mass adherence to religious practice and belief would be entirely compatible with a naturalist explanation of its origin and function.

Indeed a more nuanced relating of theology to sociology might offer some prospects that are welcome on both sides. For example, the recognition that a religiously diverse society facilitates choice and human responsibility does not always have to be the possession of secular liberalism. Several decent theological arguments were advanced in support of religious plurality in the early modern period, particularly after the traumas of the Thirty Years War. Some forms of secularism, therefore, can be seen as the upshot of distinctively religious convictions about the character of faith and religious disagreement.[14] And, second, a degree of disenchantment and differentiation of functions may help to sober some religious sensibilities and offset the potential for pathological expressions of faith. This ought to be recognized by exponents of belief. It would be hard to argue that this has not played a positive factor in the gradual decline of sectarianism in Scotland and Northern Ireland over the past generation. In the eighteenth century, the moderate philosophers and theologians in Glasgow and elsewhere recognised that some heat needed to be taken out of religious controversy if Scotland were to be pacified and to achieve a greater measure of cultural, political, and economic flourishing. The Scottish Enlightenment thus took root in Presbyterian soil, partly through this recognition and the transformation that it afforded.

For the new atheism, however, much if not all religion is treated as pathological. It is destructive of social harmony, individual responsibility, and patterns of cooperation across languages, tribes, and nations. The anthem of this movement might be John Lennon's *Imagine*.

> Imagine there's no countries
> It isn't hard to do
> Nothing to kill or die for
> And no religion too
> Imagine all the people
> Living life in peace

Within this current debate, there is also the sense amongst some public intellectuals that religion has been treated as a no-go area for robust criticism. It is suggested that the politics of tolerance, the need to integrate immigrant and religiously diverse groups into our western societies, the attempt to promote dialogue and better understanding of Islam have all contributed to a soft-centred intellectual culture that fails to engage robustly with religion.[15] Clearly this is a source of irritation if not outrage amongst many critics who have assumed for years that religion is irrational, pointless, and often highly destructive. So we are witnessing a fierce counter-attack on the part of secularism. This may explain the campaigning language of much of the literature. Dawkins writes for people who want to question religion and to find the courage to doubt publicly and openly some of the strongest convictions of their fellow-citizens. Dennett speaks about the need to 'break the spell' and so to end the taboo surrounding critical discussion of religion. He argues that atheists need to find their identity, not negatively as those who reject what others believe, but as those who have a positive and healthy account of the world and the ends of human life. A new label has even been proposed, that of 'brights'. Atheists are to be termed 'brights', people who have the wit and wisdom to reject the discredited habits and convictions of their ancestors. If believers find this term patronizing then they are invited to devise their own comeback label. Why not call yourselves 'supers', as in 'supernaturalists', suggests Dennett?[16] So you can be bright or super, it seems, but not super-bright.

This sense of heroically championing a worthy but persecuted cause may appear strange to some audiences, particularly in Europe. After all, it is not particularly difficult in our media or public institutions today to proclaim oneself a sceptic or atheist. Indeed Richard Dawkins keeps telling us that most intellectuals in this country do not bother with religion. Nevertheless, we should probably not underestimate the hostility that atheism still arouses in sections of American society, nor the particularly vicious postbags that Dawkins and others receive. Recent sociological investigation into cultural attitudes towards atheism in the USA suggests that of all outsider groups, atheists are regarded with most suspicion as a dangerous influential elite.[17] Catholics,

Jews, and now Muslims may be accommodated under the sacred canopy that bestows meaning upon public life, but non-believers can find no such acceptance in American public life. This works not so much at the level of personal persecution, but in terms of the symbolic meaning attached to principled unbelief.

However, notwithstanding this American phenomenon, it is simply not the case that in our own society the critical study of religion has become taboo. On the contrary, hardly a day passes without a journalist offering us a considered opinion on religion. We are seeing a steady annual increase in the number of school pupils presenting for certificates in Religious Studies, and despite the relative decline in those seeking ordination there are more students in university courses and degree programmes in religion than ever before. The vast majority take the subject out of a non-vocational interest. The study of religion now forms a part of the liberal arts curriculum in many universities.

We are told that it is important to have an open and critical debate about religion. However, one wonders whether the current flurry of books, debates, and blogs has really achieved this. Democratic societies are marked by informed argument and civil disagreement over these and other important issues. Yet the rhetoric employed by the new atheists is often as hostile and shrill as those of the most vehement religionists. The tone of the debate is often threatening and patronizing in ways that are sometimes counter-productive.[18] Some of the heat needs to be taken out of the discussion if we are to reach a measured and balanced account of the validity of the arguments. This we are frequently reminded is how science ought to be practised—what is required of us is a judicious weighing of the evidence, a fair consideration of alternative hypotheses, a willingness to revise and even on occasion to abandon deeply held convictions. These are the marks of the scientific spirit which need to be brought to the study of religion. Yet the recent criticism of religion is at times too rabid and disabling of patient and constructive debate. In the preface to *The God Delusion*, Richard Dawkins thanks his wife for coaxing him through all his hesitations and self-doubts. More than one critic has remarked that Mrs Dawkins must have had an easy time of it, so little sign is there of any doubt or reservation in this work.

In identifying 'the new atheism', however, we should not forget that the field is wider. There are important if less publicized thinkers who maintain a sceptical position on religion but without engaging in dismissive or vituperative attacks. They reckon the conversation worth having, not all the considerations stacking up with overwhelming force on one side. Reasonable people of good will can disagree without demonizing or sneering at the opposition. So the philosopher Thomas Nagel, while himself sceptical, argues that a debate is worth having over whether the order of the natural world and the phenomenon of human consciousness require a transcendent explanation. To see exponents of this view as on a slippery slope leading to 9/11 is just absurd.[19] Similarly, Edward O. Wilson, a leading exponent of sociobiology, claims that we do not know enough to pronounce on the truth claims of religion but we can at least recognize that it has its articulate and decent defenders. Describing himself as on the diplomatic rather than militant wing of secularism, he searches for common ground with religion.[20]

In what follows, my claim is that a conversation needs to be established between those occupying the middle ground of scepticism and faith, where each side recognizes that it has something to learn from the other whether that is about the persistence of faith or its many pathological expressions in the world. This, moreover, may be a moral imperative in today's world where international cooperation and cross-faith alliances are increasingly needed.

Notes

1. 1 Peter 3:15.
2. Charles Taylor, *A Secular Age* (Cambridge, MA: Harvard University Press, 2007), 3.
3. Benjamin Beit-Hallahim, 'Atheist: A Psychological Profile', in Michael Martin (ed.), *Cambridge Companion to Atheism* (Cambridge: Cambridge University Press, 2007), 313.
4. Tina Beattie, *The New Atheists: The Twilight of Reason and the War on Religion* (London: Darton, Longman & Todd, 2007), 9–10.
5. Edinburgh Book Festival, 19 August, 2007. For a recording of the interview see http://www.edbookfest.co.uk. Even Dawkins himself appeared to be taken aback by such fawning praise and demurred, somewhat embarrassed, that not all his readers were like her.
6. Tina Beattie's insightful critique of *Saturday* seems to miss the extent to which Perowne is uncertain and puzzled by his changing world. See *The New Atheists*, 157ff.
7. Ian McEwan, *Saturday* (London: Vintage, 2006), 276–7.
8. Philip Jenkins, *God's Continent: Christianity, Islam and Europe's Religious Crisis* (Oxford: Oxford University Press, 2007).
9. 'A special report on religion and public life', *Economist*, 3–9 November 2007, 6.
10. Peter Berger, *The Desecularization of the World: Resurgent Religion and World Politics* (Grand Rapids: Eerdmans, 1999).
11. 'A special report on religion and public life', *Economist*, 4. Figures are drawn from the World Christian Database.
12. Grace Davie, *Religion in Britain Since 1945: Believing without Belonging* (Oxford: Blackwell, 1994) and *Europe: The Exceptional Case. Parameters of Faith in the Modern World* (London: Darton, Longman & Todd, 2002).
13. See for example the discussion in David Waines, *An Introduction to Islam*, 2nd edition (Cambridge: Cambridge University Press, 2003), 173ff.
14. I have tried to argue this in *Church, State and Civil Society* (Cambridge: Cambridge University Press, 2004).
15. Note the comments on the Salman Rushdie affair and the more recent controversy over the Danish cartoons.
16. Daniel C. Dennett, *Breaking the Spell: Religion as a Natural Phenomenon* (London: Penguin, 2007), 21.

17. Penny Edgell, Joseph Gerteis, and Douglas Hartmann, 'Atheists as "Other": Moral Boundaries and Cultural Membership in American Society', *American Sociological Review* 71(2) (2006), 211–34. I owe this reference to Chuck Mathewes.
18. Interestingly, this may be less true of continental Europe, where scholars often express surprise at the intemperate nature of the new atheism in the English-speaking world. The stronger foothold of theology in mainstream intellectual life may have something to do with this. One example of this greater accord of mutual respect is the recent dialogue between the Pope and Jürgen Habermas.
19. Thomas Nagel, 'Review of Richard Dawkins' *The God Delusion*', *New Republic*, 135 (23 October 2006), 25–9. Nagel concludes that, 'Blind faith and the authority of dogma are dangerous; the view that we can make ultimate sense of the world only by understanding it as the expression of mind or purpose is not. It is unreasonable to think that one must refute the second in order to resist the first' (p. 29).
20. Interview with Brian Appleyard, *Sunday Times*, 23 December 2007.

I

ATHEISM IN HISTORICAL PERSPECTIVE

ATHEISM is a term of contested meanings. As the Greek alpha privative suggests, 'a-theism' is essentially the negation of a position. It is not surprising, therefore, that it signifies the rejection of quite different views across space and time. A passing acquaintance with the competing philosophies of the ancient world reveals that atheism is not a new phenomenon that has emerged with the rise of modern science or the European Enlightenment.

In the ancient world thinkers as divergent as Socrates and Justin Martyr were charged with atheism, yet both were far from being atheists in the contemporary sense of that term. In the case of the former, Socrates sought the purification of popular Greek religion with its multiplicity of anthropomorphic gods and goddesses. The divine was something higher, more transcendent and ineffable, to be approached by philosophy and virtuous living. For denying their gods and corrupting the youth of the city, the Athenian authorities made him drink the hemlock. Justin, a second-century apologist of the church, notes that Christians too are charged with atheism—they do not honour pagan deities, celebrate their feasts, or offer sacrifices. For this, they are regarded as dangerous and subversive. Like Socrates and Jesus before him, Justin is martyred for his faith.

This is one trend that we find in the ancient world. It is highly critical of the plurality of human-like gods that inhabit the popular imagination. These are denied in the interests of a more refined and purer concept of the eternal or the divine that informs the physical and moral universe. In his study of atheism in pagan antiquity, A. B. Drachman notes that it was restricted to elite groups of wealthy and educated philosophers. Within the ancient world, it had little purchase on societies at large.[1] This train of philosophical thought is already under way in some of the pre-Socratics such as Xenophanes. It is atheism only in the sense of denying one set of gods in order to affirm a purer form of monotheism or a monism that is distinctly religious in character.

Elsewhere in the ancient world, however, we have alternative systems of thought that more closely resemble patterns of atheism and scepticism in the modern world.[2] These include the naturalism of Democritus, who saw the universe as comprising only a set of atoms colliding at random, and also the thought of Protagoras, who seems to suggest a natural explanation for religion, morality, and society. In relation to the question of God, agnosticism seems to be his resting place.

With regard to the gods I cannot feel sure either that they are, or that they are not, nor what they are like in figure, for there are many things that hinder sure knowledge: the obscurity of the subject and the shortness of human life.[3]

That this is so vigorously contested by Plato suggests that it was a live option at the time. There are also those like Epicurus who while not denying the existence of the gods cannot find them to have any interest in or relevance to human affairs. This position, moreover, is not far from that of the sceptics such as Pyrrho. He cannot pronounce on such lofty matters as the gods and in forsaking such questions seeks a peace and contentment that unfulfilled speculative questing cannot attain. By virtue of his great philosophical poem *De Rerum*

Natura, Lucretius (*c.* 99–55 BCE) is perhaps the most complete atheist of classical times. He argues that the gods do not exist, that life ends at death, and that religion ought to be abolished because of its many misdeeds.

Each of these ancient positions adumbrates philosophies of the modern period. One conclusion that can immediately be drawn from this is that atheism does not rest upon or derive from modern experimental science. Although some forms of atheism have appealed to the methods and conclusions of modern science, a study of ancient philosophy should alert us to the ways in which the various options were established long before modernity.

In the west, atheism has come to be associated with the rejection of the God of the Christian faith, or the God of Judaeo-Christian theism, or perhaps still more broadly the God of the three Abrahamic faiths. Again it is essentially reactive, taking as its starting point the basic beliefs of a religion or society and offering a revisionist or sceptical judgement upon these. Although there are acknowledged affinities with earlier pagan philosophies, this modern atheism has its own distinct cultural context, particularly with respect to Christianity. The causes of atheism in the modern world are generally located in the culture of the Renaissance and Reformation in the fifteenth and sixteenth centuries. The list of causal factors is quite long. It includes the development of free rational enquiry independent of ecclesiastical control, the rise and progress of natural science based upon theory and experiment rather than canonical texts, the religious fracturing of Europe producing different groups with their conflicting accounts of the source and content of religious belief, the printed text and emergence of educated elites outside the church, and the steady weakening of distinctive tenets that had held firm for many centuries, particularly the belief in hell. If the reality of the next world impinged less upon human consciousness, then a greater attention must fall upon this one. Christopher Hill has suggested that while this hastened the rise of religious toleration, it must also have created a climate in which it became much easier to opt out by rejecting all forms of faith. Catholics, Lutherans, Calvinists, Baptists, Jews, and Quakers could gradually begin to learn co-existence, albeit with repeated lapses, but this climate was one in which scepticism could also flourish.[4] Not all religions could be true in everything, it was claimed, but they might all be false.

During the era of the Reformations, atheism signalled not so much the intellectual rejection of fundamental Christian beliefs as a lack of piety. The ungodly were charged with atheism on account of the practical absence of religion from their lives. This is a point that will prove significant in subsequent criticism of the new atheism. The term 'religion' in its current usage is of relatively recent origin. It is a genus of which each of the world religions is taken to be a species. Our use of the concept now tends to block adherents of faiths into discrete groups, each determined by a different set of beliefs, texts, and practices. This creates some possible difficulties in isolating the beliefs and practices of a religion from those of a broader culture. Patterns of dress and eating, forms of family and social life, and observance of rituals and festivals are all integral to religion. To sequester the more cognitive dimensions of faith as the key index to religious identity is both to ignore its broad practical context, while also imposing a homogeneity upon adherents across space and time that simply does not exist. In this respect, it is instructive to remember that the term 'religion' previously designated not so much a distinct system of belief as the practice of piety. As the Harvard historian of religion Wilfred Cantwell Smith famously argued, until the modern era the term 'religion' did not appear with an article—there were not religions in the singular and the plural. Instead religion tended to refer to the encounter with the divine, the practice of piety, and the forms of life that faith engendered. This is its meaning in Augustine and in Calvin's

classical study, *Institutes of the Christian Religion*, where the
Latin *religio* refers not so much to one world religion amongst
others but to the piety of Christian people. Arguing that the
term 'religion' evolved to isolate competing faiths in the modern world, Cantwell Smith notes how its meaning has shifted
from earlier periods.[5] It may now be a term that we cannot
do without—today's awareness of religious diversity is greater
than ever before and in many parts of the world Christians and
Muslims understand themselves in relation to each other. But,
in using it uncritically, we may be in danger of smuggling ques-
tionable assumptions into our understanding of what religion
typically involves and how it is widely expressed. At worst, it
may occlude the significant overlap and commonality across
faiths that can unite rather than divide people of sincere piety.

We should not underestimate the difficulty experienced in
earlier times by those who refused faith. It took some courage
in face of a hostile majority. As David Wooton notes, the
Reformation saw the rapid construction of an extensive vocabulary in both Latin and the vernacular to describe forms of
unbelief and impiety.[6] Heretics, deviants, and backsliders were
denounced as atheist, deist, Epicurean, libertine, and antino-
mian. In being named thus, one was perceived as a danger
to ecclesial and civic life. The existence of genuine atheists
was doubted by some. Others, like John Toland, may have
advocated deist beliefs as a way of maintaining a deep scepticism without openly promoting atheism. Persecution was not
uncommon. As late as 1697, Thomas Aikenhead, an Edinburgh divinity student, was hanged on the road to Leith for
expounding sceptical views on the authority of Scripture and
the existence of God. The case shocked John Locke and
other exponents of religious toleration. The reaction against
the Aikenhead case appears to have contributed to the more
tolerant and latitudinarian climate of Scottish moderatism in
the succeeding century. In Glasgow not long afterwards, Professor John Simson was charged by his Presbytery and the

General Assembly with teaching if not atheism then some quite surprisingly revisionist doctrines. These included: Arianism, the view that the Son of God was a creature rather than of the divine essence; Socinianism, with its more rationalist account of the work of Christ; and other assorted teachings including even the possibility that the moon was inhabited. After a protracted discussion in the courts of the Church of Scotland, Simson was suspended from teaching by the General Assembly of 1727. Nevertheless, he was allowed to remain in post and to draw his salary as Professor of Divinity. It was a 'punishment' of which academics today can only dream.[7]

What we find in the history of modern ideas is a mosaic of patterns that exhibit some chronological development roughly along the following lines. First we have the deflated and radically revisionist types of theism and forms of scepticism in the early modern period of the seventeenth century. These then lead to the more confident and self-assertive atheism of the Enlightenment in the following century. Later, as this becomes commonplace, we encounter quite nostalgic and mournful forms of unbelief in the Victorian and Edwardian periods. The rejection of religion is no longer a bracing of oneself against a strong intellectual head wind. Now it has become an irresistible trend with unstoppable momentum. And, finally, with the refusal of religion to disappear, atheism manifests itself again in the early–to–mid-twentieth century in more aggressive and strident tones. We find this style of atheism now being repeated early in the twenty-first century in the face of the global resurgence of religion. Of course, this developmental story is highly simplistic. Always there are exceptions and counter-examples readily available. Nevertheless, it does reveal that each type of atheism is reactive. It has its context to which we should remain alert. The tonal differences amongst sceptics and atheists throughout the modern period register the shifting setting in which alternative systems of belief can be advanced. This remains true today.

As the implicit denial of belief in the existence of the God of orthodox Christian faith, atheism appears to have been acknowledged at least from the time of the Reformation. It is difficult to gauge its real as opposed to imaginary presence and whether it amounted to much more than a heterodoxy of belief.[8] Leading resources for atheist reflection included the work of two distinguished early modern philosophers, Thomas Hobbes (1588–1679) and Baruch Spinoza (1632–77). In both cases, there is some ambivalence surrounding their thought and its resting place vis-à-vis the existence of God. In his political treatise *Leviathan*, Hobbes offers an argument for the existence of God and he clearly regards religion as a powerful social force. Yet the explanatory role assigned to God is minimal and he seems to view most religious beliefs as fictitious. Spinoza, a Jewish rationalist philosopher, famously identifies God with the entire natural process and so has suffered the standard charge of pantheism. His philosophy is deeply religious even while it denies the transcendence of God. Neither Hobbes nor Spinoza, therefore, can be viewed simply as atheist although they do offer lines of enquiry that depart from previous standards in their religious communities. The possibility of holding to a position in which the most fundamental elements seem either to be missing or inessential now emerges.

It is sometimes claimed that with the rise of modern science, particularly following Newton, the place for divine action and influence in the world was marginalized. No longer an admixture of natural and supernatural causes, the world now became the arena of mechanical forces. The regularity of scientific laws across space and time thus generated belief in a world that was entirely directed by natural forces. God was increasingly driven to the edge or into the ever-decreasing gaps. It was on this soil that deism flourished in the early eighteenth century. Yet research suggests that the situation was not so simple. The extent to which God was active and evident in the world largely depended on how one understood the laws of nature themselves. To what extent were these expressive of God and instrumental of divine power? John Hedley Brooke has argued that it was this latter issue, rather than the emergence of Newtonian science itself, that determined the origins of modern atheism.[9]

David Hume was both the leading figure of the Scottish Enlightenment and also its most egregious in terms of his avowal of scepticism. His attack on miracles as proof of divine revelation, his criticism of the standard arguments for the divine existence, and his account of the history of religion all tend towards a position that is sceptical and naturalist. Hume was no defender of Scottish Presbyterian faith, although many of his friends belonged to the ranks of its clergy. Yet even Hume thought it judicious to suspend the publication of his renowned *Dialogues Concerning Natural Religion* until after his death in 1776, and debate continues over the precise resting place of his views amidst the exchanges of the three protagonists. Is there still a residual puzzlement that keeps the question of God alive during the closing stages of the *Dialogues*? At face value, there appears to be, although this may only be a dramatic feature of the text. Other thinkers of the Scottish Enlightenment attributed a reduced significance to religion—Adam Smith's views are at best elusive, while Principal Robertson is often suspected of deism—yet Hume is the only thinker within this intellectual climate openly to espouse radical scepticism.

An important feature of the debates generated by Hume is the way in which it is the overall shape of his philosophy that animates religious criticism, and not merely the specific attacks on miracles or natural theology when considered in isolation. The subsequent development of the philosophy of religion as a separate compartment of study dealing with the proofs, miracles, and the problem of evil has tended to obscure this important contextual point. Hume's naturalism, particularly with respect to epistemology and morals, was an affront to a society in which religious belief and practice were central to its fabric. The inculcation of piety was necessary for its social, cultural, and economic benefits. It was also for this reason that philosophers, such as Thomas Reid, who attempted to replace Hume's scepticism with something more 'wholesome' did not feel particularly obliged to contest every argument he levelled against the specific tenets of faith.[10]

Hume once remarked that he knew no atheists. But a visit to Paris was soon to change all this. There he encountered a significant group of self-avowed atheists who regularly met and dined together. Baron d'Holbach pointed out to Hume that of the eighteen people gathered at their dinner table fifteen were atheists; the other three, he added, had yet to make up their minds.[11] The first such self-avowed atheist is often taken to be Denis Diderot (1713–84), the renowned French Encyclopaedist. (The term 'atheism' may itself have first appeared in sixteenth-century France.) It was remarked that he was a deist in the country and an atheist in Paris.[12] The workings of nature could be explained by immanent processes without recourse to the God hypothesis. Instead of rendering God a bystander, as the deists tended to do, why not deny God outright? These ideas were adopted with enthusiasm by Baron D'Holbach and others. Thus there emerges a community of atheism that takes us beyond the limits of a reactive scepticism into the development of an alternative intellectual movement that has its own distinctive outlook and practices. Rather than merely opting out of the church, there is now the possibility of opting into an alternative worldview, life-style, and community.

By the latter part of the nineteenth century, the expression of atheism has shifted again to the extent that some writers begin to treat it as an inevitable, default position. Thus it is experienced amidst wistful and nostalgic longing for an older worldview that is now receding before our eyes. This is the tenor of Matthew Arnold's poem 'Dover Beach', with the retreat of faith compared to the ebbing of the ocean tide. Thomas Hardy repeats this elegiac theme in several of his poems, most notably *God's Funeral* written around 1909.[13] Unlike the flickering hopes at the end of 'The Darkling Thrush' or 'The Oxen', where he considers the legend that the animals in the stable bowed down before the Christ child 'hoping that it might be so', Hardy no longer pretends. 'Thus dazed and puzzled,' twixt gleam and gloom/ mechanically I followed with the rest.' That jarring adverb reveals both his compulsion to participate in God's funeral and also the victory of a scientific mind-set. He follows the mourners behind God's coffin, with resignation: now there is no solace. The same mood is evoked by William Dyce's painting in 1858 of Pegwell Bay at the appearing of Donati's comet. Some isolated figures stand on the shoreline in search of ancient fossils beneath cliffs that they know to be much older than the biblical account suggests. The tide is receding to reveal an empty landscape while overhead the passing comet suggests a momentous change in human affairs.

This is wistful atheism. Contrast it with a more aggressive mode. Nietzsche's madman haunts the streets of his city reminding his fellow-citizens of the death of God. 'We have killed him—you and I! We are all his murderers . . . The holiest and mightiest thing the world has ever possessed has bled to death under our knives: who will wipe this blood from us . . . There was never a greater deed—and whoever is born after us will on account of this deed belong to a higher history than all history up to now.'[14] For Nietzsche the death of God is a moment of opportunity as well as danger. We can abandon the servile virtues of religion and liberate human beings to a fuller existence. Writing in 1882, Nietzsche argues that a shadow has been cast over Europe now that the Christian God has become unbelievable: an old morality has to be replaced by a new way of life.[15] Yet the demand for certainty, the longing for security, entails that religion is still required by most people 'in old Europe'. (Nietzsche used this expression long before Donald Rumsfeld.)[16] The craven desire to be ruled by an external authority whether in religious or some displaced secular guise is a sign of a sickening of the will. 'The less someone knows how to command, the more urgently does he desire someone who commands, who commands severely—a god, prince, the social order, doctor, father, confessor, dogma, or party conscience.'[17]

Less dramatic perhaps, but no less strident, is the tone of Bertrand Russell's outraged rejection of belief in twentieth-century Britain. In a series of polemical writings, Russell launches a full-frontal attack on the intellectual claims of faith, its historical record, and its cramping effects upon modern life. He offers an alternative creed of freedom, autonomy, and moral endeavour. Yet even in Russell there is an element of wistfulness when he writes at the start of the twentieth century. Human beings are the product of random causes, the outcome of accidental collocations of atoms. 'Only within the scaffolding of these truths, only on the firm foundation of unyielding despair, can the soul's habitation henceforth be safely built.'[18] He is happy to assume the heroic air of one who occasionally wishes that faith were true but is compelled to tell it otherwise by his commitment to the disinterested pursuit of truth. His assault would continue in less romantic prose as he attacked the record of the churches in 1927. Christianity is unreasonable. It is a religion based on fear that shackles our human freedom and opposes the progressive force of science. Its doctrines are ethically perverse and a source of misery to the human race.[19]

Russell's more combative atheism is matched on the continent by the work of existentialists such as Sartre and Camus for whom the denial of God's existence takes on positive significance. The importance of freedom, decision, and commitment is enhanced, according to Sartre, by the absence of God. Meaning has to be constructed by human beings, because there is none in the fabric of the universe. This is the rallying call of his humanistic existentialism. If God does not exist, then we must make something of ourselves. This is the condition of freedom to which we are condemned. Sartre's atheist is far from indifferent to religion: its relevance resides in its being false.[20] As Iris Murdoch notes, the valuable is not a property of the world for Sartre, our tasks are not written in the sky. This is deeply significant because it throws us back upon our own resources: meaning has to be constructed by human beings in a godless universe.[21] There is a dramatic quality to this rejection of belief which sets it apart from the more urbane dismissal of religion in much Anglo-American philosophy. Sartre's atheism also recalls us to the practical features of religious commitment. According to all faith traditions, a lively belief in God is integral to a broader set of intellectual, practical, and emotional commitments. It is not merely a proposition to which one assents, as one might for example believe that there is life on Mars. Conversely, the rejection of religion may not simply be a matter of indifference or incredulity when presented with a particular set of beliefs, although this is surely how it is for many people much of the time in western societies today. The non-existence of God is not just believed—it is positively willed. Hence, a turning away from religion may itself be a strong emotional decision in the face of beliefs and commitments that one rejects, perhaps on moral grounds. In Dostoevsky's great novel, Ivan Karamazov speaks passionately of handing his ticket back to God. His rejection of his brother's faith is born not of an inability to believe but of a conscious decision to turn away from a particular vision of life. The suffering of children demands no less of him.[22]

Some thinkers have sought to introduce a sharp distinction between atheism and agnosticism. The latter term is more recent in provenance, having been introduced by Thomas Huxley in the nineteenth century to describe a form of scepticism that simply acknowledged the limitations of the human intellect in face of metaphysical questions.[23] Having refused all the available 'isms' of his days, Huxley invented his own so that, as he later said, like all the other foxes he too could have a tail.

The term 'agnosticism' is of course useful in designating a position in which belief in the existence or non-existence of God is suspended. We might reasonably reach the position that the evidence is inconclusive or that the reach of our intellects is far too limited to pronounce on such an issue. Nevertheless, the line between atheism and agnosticism is too blurred for this to be a sharp and useful distinction except in some restricted contexts. In stressing our inability to pronounce on such lofty matters, Hume might be described as an agnostic or sceptic rather than an atheist. Nevertheless, the naturalist worldview that he espouses is practically identical to that of atheism. God has no role to play in explaining the world and human experience, or the phenomena of art, morality, and religion. Hence a strong agnosticism tends to merge with a practical atheism whereby the concept of God becomes redundant in explaining or expressing features of the world and human existence. There is less of a sharp divide than a spectrum of views ranging at one end from passionate conviction through degrees of tentativeness, suspension of judgement, indifference, and scepticism to outright hostility and dismissal. While it is easier to locate articulate intellectual elites on this spectrum, it may be harder to reach conclusions about the wider population. Even in times of apparent widespread religious affiliation, there must have been degrees of enthusiasm and credulity. Getting inside people's heads and hearts is not a straightforward exercise.

Recent social-scientific research has investigated the prevalence of atheism in the modern world. Today it is estimated there may be around 500 million atheists in the world, making it the equivalent of the fourth largest religion, after Christianity, Islam, and Hinduism.[24] In their 2004 study, Norris and Inglehart report that the western democracies of Europe,

Canada, and Australia tend to display higher levels of explicit disbelief than is found in other parts of the world.[25] This supports the conclusion favoured by exponents of the secularization thesis that under conditions of increased prosperity, security, health, and material satisfaction, religious belief and practice suffer decline. One exception merits comment—the USA, where levels of belief and practice remain much higher than in most other western countries. Norris and Inglehart attempt to explain this by reference to the higher degree of economic insecurity in the USA compared to other countries in the west. Since this is rife in the USA, religion continues to flourish. In other words, to save the thesis, the richest country in the world has now to be reclassified as amongst the poorest, at least in this one respect. This seems prima facie implausible, if only because a great many rich people in the USA are found in church each Sunday. How else can one explain the resources and power commanded by evangelical Christianity? In the past, much of the literature on secularization concentrated on American exceptionalism. Now, however, it is Europe, especially western and central Europe, that is regarded as an exception by comparison with the rest of the world. Instead of appealing merely to economic factors, recent theorists have focused on history, law, education, welfare, and the relationship of church to state to explore in greater depth the causes of the religious differences between western Europe and the USA.[26] What emerges is less a thesis to explain the peculiarity of America than one that accounts for the distinctiveness of parts of modern Europe. Viewed in this way, secularization is no longer perceived as an inevitable outcome of modernization.

Theologians have sometimes offered accounts of atheism that seek to explain this as a reaction to mistaken constructions of religion. The strategy here has been to accept the criticism but to plead that the target is misplaced. The less plausible of these strategies tend to identify a bogeyman who has set western thought and civilization off on the wrong track. In naming his mistakes, we can see why atheism flourished and why it was a legitimate rejection of an aberration. Several candidates have presented themselves for this role of intellectual bogeyman, but there is no consensus as to who the most likely suspect is. These include Kant (for his rejection of realism), Descartes (for his turn to the subject), Luther (for the subjectivism of his Reformation), and most recently Duns Scotus (for his thesis about the univocity of being which allegedly places God within the same frame of reference as the natural world). Roughly speaking, the strategy is to propose that we expose the error and convict the culprit before then retrieving some older, more pristine worldview that will not be vulnerable to later forms of scepticism. The destruction of idols can thus be welcomed in the service and worship of the one true God. Without entering into detailed discussion of these hypotheses, they can be treated with a good deal of circumspection for several reasons. History is not readily divided into epochs determined by the intellectual constructions of great men. Each thinker has a context to which he or she is indebted. The emergence of new ideas, theories, and philosophies can never be explained in mono-causal terms. Always there are multiple explanations of different types. Every system of thought, moreover, borrows heavily from earlier constructions and is not easily detached in such a way as to attract praise or blame in such unmixed quantities. In any case, the radical criticism of religion such as is found in Hume and Kant will not easily be deflected by the claim that they are merely attacking a false set of gods in whom no-one really believed. Atheism may sometimes be guilty of distortion, but it cannot readily be trumped by the retrieval of a medieval worldview, Platonic philosophy, or Biblical positivism. The criticisms need to be faced and not sidestepped by such intellectual manoeuvres.

The most sophisticated theological discussion of atheism has been that of Michael Buckley. His study *At the Origins of*

Modern Atheism (1987) claims that Christian theologians invited and encouraged attack by shifting position some time during the early modern period. Instead of grounding faith in religious experience, attempts to establish it on philosophical and scientific grounds merely exposed it to further hostile attack. As thinkers sought to prove God's existence, as if this was a necessary pre-condition of faith, so it became easier to undermine it by dismantling the proofs. In this respect, the origin of atheism is found in the self-alienation of religion itself. He notes the extent to which theologians such as Marin Mersenne in the first half of the seventeenth century became embroiled in establishing faith claims on philosophical grounds, as opposed to confronting their opponents with what was vital to religion. As a result, he says, 'the fundamental reality of Jesus as the embodied presence and witness of the reality of God within human history was never brought into the critical struggle of Christianity in the next three hundred years.'[27] Yet Buckley's timely reminder of what is vital to Jewish and Christian faith does not itself abolish the project of natural theology. There remains the need to show how all human enquiry points towards God and how the different disciplines can exhibit a unity that is comprehended by religion.[28] The 'proof' of God lies within the act of faith, but this does not absolve theology from the responsibility of attending to the claims of atheism. Following Buckley, it might even be claimed that modern theology has been shaped by a prevailing culture of disbelief since the Enlightenment. Troubled by the scepticism of its surrounding culture, it has turned anxiously to apologetic strategies to legitimate and commend the fundamental claims of religion before its cultured despisers.

Our short tour of western atheism has revealed a largely reactive but increasingly self-confident demeanour. This is true a fortiori of the new atheism. It registers, often intemperately, its rage at the continued prevalence of religion in the contemporary world, coupled with an incredulity concerning its standard claims and practices. A liberating humanist alternative is at hand and is confidently asserted as providing a more rational and fulfilling way of life. Human societies can flourish and live well without religion, it is held, albeit as a tenet of faith since this is not yet empirically confirmed. And like earlier forms of scepticism, it offers some arguments against the core beliefs of theism while also seeking to offer a natural explanation of the phenomenon of religion itself. These arguments and explanations require careful examination.

Notes

1. A. B. Drachman, *Atheism in Pagan Antiquity* (London: Gylendal, 1922), 146ff.
2. For further discussion see James Thrower, *Western Atheism: A Short History* (New York: Prometheus Books, 2000).
3. Protagoras, *Concerning the Gods*, fragment 4, quoted by Thrower, *Western Atheism*, 30.
4. Christopher Hill, 'Tolerance in Seventeenth-Century England: Theory and Practice', in Susan Mendus (ed.), *The Politics of Toleration* (Edinburgh: Edinburgh University Press, 1999), 38ff.
5. Wilfred Cantwell Smith, *The Meaning and End of Religion* (London: SPCK, 1978), 37.
6. David Wootton, 'New Histories of Atheism', in Michael Hunter & David Wooton (eds.), *Atheism from the Reformation to the Enlightenment* (Oxford: Oxford University Press, 1992), 25 (13–54)
7. See the discussion of Simson in H. B. M. Reid, *The Divinity Professors in the University of Glasgow* (Glasgow, 1923), 204–40 and Ian Hazlett, 'Ebbs and Flows of Theology in Glasgow, 1451–1843', in W. I. P. Hazlett (ed.), *Traditions of Theology in Glasgow 1450–1990* (Edinburgh: Scottish Academic Press, 1993), 1–26.
8. This is explored by David Wootton, 'New Histories of Atheism'.

9. John Hedley Brooke, 'Natural Law in the Natural Sciences: the Origins of Modern Atheism?', *Science and Christian Belief*, 4 (1992), 83–103.

10. I owe this insight to Professor Sandy Stewart. See M. A. Stewart, 'Rational Religion and Common Sense', in Joseph Houston (ed.), *Thomas Reid: Context, Influence and Significance* (Edinburgh: Dunedin Academic Press, 2004), 123–60.

11. This story has several variants. It is recorded by Ernest Mossner, *The Life of David Hume*, 2nd edition (Oxford: Oxford University Press, 1980), 483.

12. See Thrower, *Western Atheism*, 106.

13. Hardy's atheism is discussed in the opening chapter of A. N. Wilson, *God's Funeral* (London: John Murray, 1999).

14. *The Gay Science*, ed. Bernard Williams (Cambridge: Cambridge University Press, 2001), 120.

15. Ibid., 199.

16. Ibid., 205.

17. Ibid., 206.

18. *A Free Man's Worship* (London: Unwin, 1976).

19. See Bertrand Russell, *Why I Am Not a Christian* (London: Unwin, 1957).

20. Jean-Paul Sartre, *Existentialism and Humanism* (London: Methuen, 1948), 27ff.

21. Iris Murdoch, *Sartre: Romantic Rationalist* (London: Collins, 1967), 66.

22. This is explored by Stewart R. Sutherland in *Atheism and the Rejection of God: Contemporary Philosophy and the Brothers Karamazov* (Oxford: Blackwell, 1977).

23. 'Most of my colleages [sic] were -*ists* of one sort or another; and however kind and friendly they might be, I, the man without a rag of a label to cover himself with could not fail to have some of the uneasy feelings which must have beset the historical fox when, after leaving the trap in which his tail remained, he presented himself to his normally elongated companions. So I took thought, and invented what I conceived to be the appropriate title of 'agnostic'. It came into my head as suggestively antithetic to the 'gnostic' of Church history, who professed to know so much about the very things of which I was ignorant.' *Collected Essays*, vol. v (London: Macmillan, 1894), 239.

24. See Phil Zuckerman, 'Atheism: Contemporary Numbers and Patterns', in Michael Martin (ed.), *Cambridge Companion to Atheism* (Cambridge: Cambridge University Press, 2004), 47–65.
25. Pippa Norris and Ronald Inglehardt, *Sacred and Secular: Religion and Politics Worldwide* (Cambridge: Cambridge University Press, 2004).
26. See Peter Berger, Grace Davie, and Effie Fokas, *Religious America, Secular Europe? A Theme and Variations* (Aldershot: Ashgate, 2008).
27. Michael Buckley, *At the Origins of Modern Atheism* (New Haven: Yale University Press, 1987), 67.
28. Ibid., 360f.

2

THE CREDIBILITY OF RELIGIOUS BELIEF: CLAIMS AND COUNTER-CLAIMS

Much of our contemporary intellectual culture remains in a default setting of rationalism and disenchantment. The sea of faith has seemingly receded leaving the beach empty of evidence for God's existence. Within the new atheism, there is no inclination to re-open the case for God, only a determination to reiterate and reinforce a raft of familiar arguments. These include the following claims: the standard arguments for divine existence are weak and almost entirely lacking in validity; the increasingly successful explanatory power of the natural sciences renders theological explanation redundant; and the counter-evidence of evil tells decisively against any relevant form of theism. Each of these claims shall be inspected in this chapter.

Before engaging this debate, however, some remarks on the nature of faith are required. Much of the discussion assumes that religious belief is settled one way or another by a weighing of the evidence for and against God's existence. At its most crude, this can sometimes construe faith as if it were analogous to belief in extra-terrestrials, the Loch Ness monster, or wild cats in the Scottish highlands. These elusive creatures are held by some to exist but are doubted by others. Our belief will or ought to be determined in proportion to our judgement regarding the available evidence. Richard Dawkins writes in this way when he employs Bertrand Russell's parable of the celestial teapot. If we liken God to a small teapot somewhere between the earth and Mars that orbits the sun, then the question of its existence might be settled by the use of telescopes. If the object is too small to be detected by conventional means that we can establish new tests. But if no test offers any evidence of the teapot then we can reasonably conclude that it does not exist. This might be overturned by subsequent evidence, but for the time being it is the rational position to adopt.[1]

Yet belief in God's existence seldom functions in this way. There must be few persons who come to faith through a weighing of the probabilities for and against God as a super-celestial object. While one should not exclude this possibility out of hand, it seems that faith seldom arises through a probability calculation that God's existence is above 0.5 on a scale from zero to one. Several features of faith render this scenario unlikely. It is not so much a judgement about one object amidst many others in the universe but more a conviction about how the entire universe is to be regarded. Is it the expression of some transcendent purpose, suffused with a meaning that we apprehend only partially? Or is it a brute physical fact that has arisen without explanation or sense beyond that which we ourselves create? Expressed in this sort of language, a faith commitment is not ventured or refused in the same way as a hypothesis about an object in our solar system. Religious belief has an organizational power that is not shared by most other belief states. It determines thought, emotion, and action in ways that reshape perception of the world and our place in it. To this extent, philosophers of religion have been correct to point to the peculiar features of religious language and the forms of life they facilitate. Belief in God is quite different from belief in other things. It is neither settled by appeal to agreed standards of evidence, nor is the role of faith removed in the unlikely event of attaining complete certainty with respect to the putative facts. This might explain Wittgenstein's enigmatic comment 'that if there were evidence this would in fact destroy the whole business'.[2] The difference between belief and unbelief is more like that between a picture which is constantly in the foreground for some people but is not used at all by others.[3] Alternatively, to change the metaphor, one might see it as a set of tools used by some while discarded or ignored or unknown by others. There is of course support for this from the theological traditions of the church, especially Lutheranism, which stress the vital element of 'fiducia' (trust) in the act of faith. As personal trust it involves a reorientation of the entire self and not merely the addition of one more belief to our cognitive stock. Theologians often complement this with an account of grace that construes faith not only as an activity of the human person but as that person's apprehension by the Spirit of God. In this way, the act of faith requires a comprehensive intellectual and practical reshaping of the self.

In appreciating the transformative nature of faith, moreover, one can also recognize that belief is only one element therein. For some, this might be largely unreflective and seldom, if ever, given conceptual expression. The practice of a religion involves typically an array of customs, rituals, ethical commitments, and celebration of festivals. Usually these are of a communal nature. They can be entered into sincerely and with varying degrees of enthusiasm, even when relatively little attention may be given to the beliefs that they presuppose or symbolically express. Some propositional expressions may be a necessary condition of the meaningfulness of these practices, yet there is much more going on in religion than merely an individual's assent to a set of contested beliefs. This is not sufficiently registered by recent critics who tend to assume that religion is more or less equivalent to a collection of beliefs about the supernatural.

A good example of this is Richard Dawkins' incomprehension in considering the faith of his friend Lord Winston. Defending his commitment to Judaism, Winston has remarked that it enables him to discipline and structure his life in ways that he finds beneficial. In assessing this, however, Dawkins immediately dismisses it as quite irrelevant since it has not 'the smallest bearing on the truth value of any of its supernatural claims'.[4] Yet this is to miss Winston's point. According to its practitioners, the truthfulness of a religion is best known in living it. When it enables one to live well, this will be a strong reason for judging that some of its deepest convictions contain a measure of truth. 'By their fruits, ye shall know them.'

Recognition that faith is a high-level commitment offering an interpretation of all the available phenomena casts some doubt on evidentialist strategies of justification. These require religious belief to be rationally grounded through deductive or inductive links to more fundamental beliefs that do not themselves require such justification. Such foundational beliefs may be regarded as self-evident, incorrigible, or as universally held, unlike more particular and contested religious beliefs. One difficulty with this strategy, apart from its execution, is that there is an obvious mismatch with the ways in which faith is actually generated and sustained in lives displaying the theological virtues of faith, hope, and love. In reaction to this, philosophers such as Alvin Plantinga and Nicholas Wolterstorff in the USA—both working within a Protestant theological context—have argued that religious beliefs are properly basic in their own right. We are entitled to hold them as fundamental ways of perceiving and acting in the world without requiring their justification by links to more fundamental belief states. This position, it seems to me, has the attraction of being more appropriate to the ways in which people actually come to faith and persist in it, particularly those who acquire it through their family upbringing. As a characterization of the dynamics of religious belief it works better than more rationalist accounts.

In this respect, it seeks to retrieve a standard approach to the concept of faith that is found in pre-modern theology. Nevertheless, it requires some qualification on several counts. First, the task of specifying religious beliefs will require to be undertaken by reference to agreed sources and norms. Religious beliefs are complex, requiring elaboration and conceptual expression. This will entail a use of reason, argument, and a weighing of alternatives that ensures that religious belief is not a simple and unalterable given, as for example belief in the external world or other minds. Second, religious beliefs vary and are contested by some. In the presence of conflicting beliefs, it is necessary to appraise one's own in a way that is not generally required for more universally agreed judgements, e.g. the perception of medium-sized physical objects. Hence, the critical inspection of religious beliefs must have its place.

As a form of religious self-description, theology is charged with describing its cognitive claims. And in entering the public domain, therefore, faith is assailed by criticism and burdened with a responsibility of engaging in counter-criticism and argument. Alvin Plantinga, of course, recognizes this in his requirement that religious faith 'defeat its defeaters'. To this extent, it is incumbent upon the apologist to defend her position against attack, perhaps through in turn challenging the presuppositions and coherence of the position occupied by the critic. Nevertheless, the language of 'defeating the defeaters' suggests that somehow faith, if successful in this engagement, will be unaltered by this intellectual encounter. This seems highly unlikely. Debates with the natural sciences, historical criticism, and other faith traditions will for much of the time result in a restatement, revision, and adjustment of earlier theological positions. In this respect, theology is never immobile. There is no single confessional position that is immune to change. To assume that theology reached its zenith in the fourth, thirteenth, or seventeenth century, as Orthodox, Roman Catholic, and Protestant Christians have sometimes been tempted to do, is merely to ignore the problems of modernity and the seriousness with which these need to be tackled. T. S. Eliot's dictum that 'Christianity is always adapting itself into something that can be believed' might seem expedient or even cynical, but it contains a vital element of truth. A balance then requires to be struck between acknowledging the particular role fulfilled by faith commitments while also engaging in an ad hoc manner with the description and defence of strategic beliefs that seem to be presupposed by those same commitments.

There are two popular and well-worn arguments for God's existence. These are now the staple diet of higher and A-level syllabuses in the philosophy of religion and are covered extensively in almost all the textbooks. The standard considerations having been carefully represented for several centuries, it is difficult to do more than merely rehearse these again. One of the problems surrounding these proofs is that they tend to be taught in a rather timeless manner, lacking context and specificity. A brief study of the history of natural theology, however, reveals that different versions of the proofs have their particular location. Natural theology too has a socio-religious context that varies strikingly across cultures. The textbook analysis of the logical structure of the classical proofs (ontological, cosmological, and design) tends to obscure this. Brooke and Cantor demonstrate this by citing the example of Al-Ghazali in late-eleventh-century Baghdad.[5] His exposition of the kalam cosmological argument is still widely discussed and used in educational contexts. Yet for Al-Ghazali this was not an abstract piece of philosophizing, or an attempt to establish a foundational claim for the divine existence. It was prompted by the threat to Islamic theology posed by Aristotelian claims for the eternity of the universe. A cosmos created and governed by the personal will of God required a beginning, he believed. Hence Al-Ghazali advanced arguments that were intended to protect some of the most

cherished convictions of his religious community in the face of
pagan incursions. Or to take a more local example, M. A. Stewart has shown that the merging of the cosmological and design
arguments in early–eighteenth-century Scotland was intended
not primarily to refute atheism but to contest forms of deism
that lacked any sense of divine providence and benevolence
directing human affairs. In engaging with deist writers, the
thinkers of the early Scottish Enlightenment employ a series of
arguments intended not only to establish the divine existence
but to ascribe to God attributes that are more consistent with
the traditional claims of Christianity. The modern ahistori-
cal treatment of the proofs tends to obscure this important
function.[6] In fusing cosmological and design arguments, what
emerges is not only a first cause but also a providential ruler
of the universe who can be relied upon to order nature and
history. The particular work for which the argument is constructed will determine its shape and content.

According to the cosmological argument, the existence of
the world in general is to be explained by a self-sufficient, eternal creator who brings the universe into being. The existence
of God, thus conceived, is the answer to the ancient question
'why is there something rather than nothing?' One might point
out that this is not a question that science can answer since
it is of a different order from scientific explanation. Every
scientific account of a phenomenon must appeal to a previous
state of affairs or set of events or causal conditions. But the
more fundamental metaphysical question of why there is a
world at all is not one that is appropriate to natural science.
In face of this argument, we find Dawkins and others offering
three types of response. First, perhaps the universe is all that
there is. It lacks an explanation beyond itself and is merely a
brute fact. Second, even if we postulate God as the cause of
the universe we are left with the conundrum of who created
God? The idea of an uncaused, self-sufficient being itself raises
questions so why not stop with the world as the terminal point

of explanation? Third, it may be that there is some hidden physical explanation of the initial singularity from which our universe emerges at the big bang. This would offer a scientific answer to the question why the world exists. A critic such as Peter Atkins will claim that the 'why' question has no meaning beyond these limits.

Then we have the design argument. It is the most popular and intuitive form of reasoning in defence of the divine existence and proceeds from the order, variety, and harmony that we see displayed in the world around us. The regular movement of the planets, the intricacy of organs such as the eye in which all the parts interlock for the proper functioning of the whole, and the ways in which species are so well adapted to their environment all attest, it was claimed, a wisdom and design that have been superimposed upon the cosmos. We cannot but marvel at the organization, complexity, and beauty of the natural world. Our minds and spirits are drawn towards the idea of a Creator who calls this into being and rules it by a benign providence. As Psalm 19:1 tells us, 'the heavens are telling the glory of God and the firmament proclaims his handiwork'.

The design argument has flourished at different periods of history but it was particularly prevalent in the eighteenth and early nineteenth centuries as knowledge of the natural world began to expand. Nowadays, however, the natural sciences have an even more powerful narrative to offer of how our world has emerged and reached its present form. It tells us about an original big bang of unimaginable violence from an initial singularity about 12 billion years ago. From the expansion produced by this big bang, a process in which galaxies, stars, and planets evolved over vast distances was realized. Here within our solar system, one of many millions in our galaxy alone, carbon-based life forms have gradually emerged over hundreds of millions of years. Changes in these life forms, moreover, can be explained by patterns of survival, adaptation, and evolution within an environment that itself undergoes significant changes. In the case of human beings, our existence has emerged over about five million years from earlier hominid life forms through the neo-Darwinian principles of genetic mutation and natural selection. This is all clearly set out in scientific textbooks, popular TV programmes, and exhibitions such as that at the Natural History Museum in London.

What this shows is that much that was believed and taught for many centuries largely on the basis of Biblical evidence is manifestly false. The world was not created in its present form in six days of twenty-four-hour intervals. It is more than 6,000 years old, and the geological and biological changes that have taken place on the planet are not to be explained by reference to a single catastrophic event such as the flood. Moreover, the human species did not descend from a single, perfect pair but has evolved over a long period of time from earlier kindred species that no longer inhabit the planet.

One of the great achievements of Richard Dawkins is to have presented in a persuasive and compelling manner this scientific narrative through a series of popular texts. As someone untrained in the natural sciences, I have learned a great deal from these. He is also pretty adroit at disposing of the claims of creation scientists and intelligent design theorists who believe that evolutionary science and religion are on a collision course and that the former must be resisted for the sake of the latter. To a large extent, this is an American debate but Dawkins offers a robust and persuasive defence of Darwinian evolution. In some ways, it would suit him very well if all Christians were creationists, and at times he writes as if this were almost the case. Then there would be a swift knock-down set of rebuttals that would close the debate. If science and religion are mutually exclusive forms of explanation that compete with one another, then the vindication of science will thereby refute all religious claims.

The proper religious response to this evolutionary narrative, however, is not one of rejection but accommodation. And indeed we find this happening very soon after the appearance of Darwin's *Origin of Species* in 1859. A world evolving into new patterns, manifesting emergent properties and producing increasingly complex life forms is not inconsistent with religious explanation. Perhaps this is the way that God does it. The Creator produces an amazingly diverse, varied, and evolving web of life forms whose richness, beauty, and value attest a providential design. In any case, the intelligibility of a universe that conforms to the interdependent laws of science is itself something that science must assume. It cannot explain adequately why the universe is so rational and amenable to powerful scientific description such as big-bang cosmology or neo-Darwinian science. In this respect, the design hypothesis remains as a possible explanation that does not so much compete with the natural sciences as complement them. It cannot be made redundant or ruled out of court by the advance of science.

For this reason, it has been proposed by a number of scientists and philosophers that the explanatory accounts of religion and science are non-competitive. These belong to different domains so that we have in Stephen Jay Gould's expression 'non-overlapping magisteria' (NOMA).[7] With different conceptualities and types of description, these deal with distinct questions that cannot be satisfactorily addressed by any one institution. Recognition of these multiple conceptualities is necessary to attain wisdom, and here Gould explicitly recalls a central theme of the Hebrew Scriptures. Or, to use the metaphor advanced in debate by the geneticist Steve Jones, the battle between science and religion resembles that between a shark and a tiger. On its home ground, each is victorious, but place one within the domain of another and it will be hopelessly defeated. We need to think of them as different and intrinsically complementary. For this reason, we might view both creationism and scientific dismissals of religion as wrong-headed. Gould claims that the business of life is so complex and multi-faceted that we need the help of different magisteria in science, the arts, ethics, and religion. Critics point out that the principle of NOMA is over-worked, if it intends hermetically to seal science and religion from any contact or interaction with one another. Yet this does not appear to be Gould's intention for he notes the need to integrate magisteria in the search for wisdom.[8] Although the magisteria do not overlap, they are in intimate contact with one another. 'Science and religion interdigitate in patterns of complex fingering, and at every fractal scale of self-similarity.'[9] So there are areas of fruitful metaphysical and ethical interaction.

As already noted, there is one version of the design argument that puts it beyond the reach of science, so to speak. This is the claim that the intelligibility of the world as presupposed by the natural sciences is to be explained in terms of theological design. Richard Swinburne describes this as an argument from temporal rather than spatial order.[10] It is not so much that the world exhibits one particular structure or shape that requires explanation. Instead its conformity to scientific description, whatever this may turn out to be, is what is to be explained by natural theology. This is a presupposition rather than a product of scientific activity, and in seeking to explain it the philosopher or theologian offers a complementary level of description that functions in a different way. Of course, this does not guarantee its validity but it does instructively indicate one way in which science and religion have their separate domains. Similar remarks could be made about the cosmological claim that religion addresses the question why there is a world at all. Again the enterprise of science seems to presuppose the existence of phenomena awaiting description and explanation. It is hard to see how these could be accounted for except in terms of appeal to other states, events, or material forces, thus merely postponing the fundamental question of why there is anything at all. In this respect, the cosmological argument too functions at a complementary level from that of the natural sciences. It is a different type of explanation, rather than one that competes head-on with the sciences in a zero-sum game. It simply will not do to assert that once science has finished its job, there is no need to explore these broader metaphysical issues or to assert blithely that these are pseudo-questions. Both the enterprise and findings of science raise questions about origins and meaning that lie beyond its parameters. These have been of perennial fascination to human beings in different cultures and traditions. To dismiss them out of hand is to occupy an unduly positivist outlook that fails to engage with issues that inevitably re-present themselves.

By contrast, the project of creation science in both its Christian and Islamic forms is to situate religious truth in the same domain as that of natural science resulting in a contest between rival forms of explanation. Here there is only one winner and it is not religion. The attempt to invoke a literalist reading of Genesis 1–11 or portions of the Qur'an against the collective findings of *inter alia* cosmology, geology, palaeontology, and evolutionary biology is a hopelessly doomed enterprise, but one that is in any case quite unnecessary for the sake of maintaining the integrity of theological explanation. The case against creationism will not be rehearsed here. It is overwhelmingly strong and well documented.[11] It is sufficient to note that a proper account of the scope of scientific explanation will help us see that evolutionary biology is not ideologically loaded in favour of atheism or any other metaphysical position.

There are, however, other recent variants of the cosmological and design arguments that do place these in closer conversation with the natural sciences. These appeal respectively to the big bang and to the anthropic principle. In the case of big-bang cosmology it is argued, in a manner reminiscent of the kalam cosmological argument, that the universe has a temporal beginning about 12 billion years ago that can only be explained by reference to divine causal action. Paul Copan and William Lane Craig argue that the best scientific evidence leads to the conclusion that the universe had a beginning from an initial singularity that cannot be accounted for scientifically. On the basis of thermodynamics and the expansion of the cosmos, we cannot avoid the conclusion that the universe originated. To put the point negatively, we cannot say that it did not have a beginning or that it is eternal. It is argued that scientific attempts to avoid this conclusion—Stephen Hawking's *A Brief History of Time* is the best known example—are expressive of a metaphysical or ideological hostility to the notion of a cosmic beginning.[12] More cautiously expressed, Craig's argument is that there is nothing in big-bang cosmology that contradicts the theological account of creation out of nothing. A more speculative version of that argument would claim that the cosmology actually generates that theological doctrine. Here however there are grounds for caution. The simple claim that the universe is uncaused is not one that is readily refuted on philosophical grounds, even if neither theologians nor scientists find it appealing. Alternatively, one might appeal to some hidden physical processes that are as yet unknown to us or are in principle unknowable from our vantage point. And third, as we shall presently see, one might invoke the hypothesis of a multiverse.

In the case of the anthropic principle, it is claimed that the fundamental physical constants of the universe determined by the big bang are fine-tuned to ensure an anthropic or biocentric universe. This appeal to 'cosmic coincidences' cites such phenomena as the rate of expansion following the big bang, the subsequent chemical ingredients of the universe, and the calibration of the forces of nature. For example, if the universe had expanded at a rate greater or less than it did by even one part in a million either matter would have been strewn outwards too quickly for stars to form or else too slowly resulting in a contraction with the same effect. A cosmos that produces stars, planets, and carbon-based life forms apparently requires a very precise structure. The fact that ours exhibits exactly this leads to the conclusion that it has been finely tuned for the sake of producing life forms such as our own. Martin Rees, the Astronomer Royal, argues that a universe capable of producing galaxies and life forms must have a set of physical constants determined by six numbers.[13] Two of these govern atomic forces, two fix the size and texture of the cosmos, and two determine the properties of space itself. Had any of these six numbers been fractionally different we would not have a recipe for a universe with stars and life. That our cosmos manifests these exact constants is a remarkable fact requiring explanation. Rees suggests that either this is a brute fact without explanation, or it is a work of divine providence, or it must be the result of their being multiple universes. Others, however, have moved quite quickly to draw theological conclusions from this appearance of fine-tuning.

The anthropic principle can be advanced in either its strong or weak form. Its stronger form claims that there is only one universe, with a striking inbuilt bias towards the evolution of life forms. The term 'anthropic' may overstate the argument since these life forms may not be co-extensive with Homo sapiens. Nevertheless, we are talking here about intelligent, conscious life forms of which human beings are one possible instantiation. The weak anthropic principle claims much less, holding merely that for a universe to be observed and understood scientifically by its conscious inhabitants it will have to be one rather like ours in terms of its fundamental constants.

Recent debate around the anthropic principle has been preoccupied with the hypothesis of a multiverse. This has generated considerable discussion amongst cosmologists and particle physicists. It would be a mistake to regard it merely as the invention of extravagant metaphysicians. The concept of a multiverse is of many universes rather than one, although this requires quite careful explication. There are three ways in which the concept has been construed but I shall deal here only with the first.[14]

(i) There is the spatial notion of a multiple universe comprising different sub-regions of a single, infinite space. These might be likened to bubbles of space-time that are causally disconnected from each other. Our own cosmos from the big bang onwards is simply one such bubble amongst very many others.

(ii) Second, we might think of a temporal multiverse in which there are consecutive bounces or cycles of a single, oscillating space-time. According to this conceptual formulation, our universe is merely one phase of this multiverse which begins with a big bang and ends with a crunch. Other phases may be very different in terms of their physical parameters. There are difficulties, however, with this conception of a multiverse on account of the principle of entropy.

(iii) Third, we might think more speculatively of a multiplicity of universes that do not belong to the same space-time. Perhaps by invoking quantum mechanics and its notion of possible worlds we can see an endless number of universes splitting and diverging from this one. In turn, this one may itself be regarded as only one amongst a potentially infinite number, all possible options being realized.

The first of these options is tentatively proposed by several physicists, including Rees himself who suggests ways in which an ensemble of universes might have evolved, only one of which has the physical structure of our own. He argues that our conception of the physical universe has increased spectacularly over the last few centuries so we should not baulk at a further enlargement that accommodates the idea of a multiverse. While the principle of economy seems to militate against this, Rees claims that the multiverse hypothesis may eventually prove to be scientifically fruitful. So go easy with Ockham's razor, he advises.[15]

Whichever version we prefer, a consequence of this postulation of multiple domains, each manifesting a different physical structure, is that the strong anthropic principle becomes a weak one. It is not that ours is the only domain, the peculiarly biocentric bias of which requires explanation. Instead, given the multiplicity of such domains, it is no surprise that one has emerged like ours and that we are here to observe it. Our universe is an oasis within an otherwise sterile multiverse. A plurality of worlds, as David Hume long ago suggested, can then remove the need to appeal to design to explain the particular features of this one. Rees illustrates this point nicely by likening the multiverse to a large 'off the shelf' clothes shop. Given the size of the stock in store, we should not be surprised to find one suit that fits us perfectly. 'Likewise, if our universe is selected from a multiverse, its seemingly designed or fine-tuned features wouldn't be surprising.'[16] The analogy just about works, although if you are unusually large or small you might not find anything that fits you.

There is, however, a possible rejoinder. A generating process that enables multiple domains, at least one of which is like ours, itself requires to be explained. Why our multiverse should have a principle of generation that renders probable or inevitable at least one anthropic universe itself requires explanation since it does not appear to be obviously right or at all self-explanatory. As one recent writer puts it, 'even if an inflationary multiverse-generator exists, it must involve just the right combination of laws, principles and fields for the production of life-permitting universes'.[17] It is not clear how science could investigate why one generating process was instantiated rather than another. This seems in principle to be beyond any measurable phenomena, and here again a transcendent design hypothesis can gain some purchase, a conclusion that Paul Davies reaches in his discussion of the multiverse in *The Goldilocks Enigma*.[18]

So while a multiverse theory certainly weakens the anthropic principle, it is not clear whether the hypothesis can render theological explanation redundant. If we have an ensemble of universes that is amenable to scientific description and which is capable of generating one like ours, then we can reasonably ask whether this requires explanation. The ensemble is not any more self-explanatory than one single universe. A multiverse that is rationally intelligible is almost as much in need of explanation as our universe alone, even if it lacks a single anthropic bias. It will continue to display a rational structure which in principle is capable of scientific investigation and description. For some physicists, the hypothesis is situated so far beyond the reach of scientific understanding that it remains at the level of speculation or fantasy.[19] It has even been said, perhaps unfairly, that the multiverse is the last refuge of the atheist.[20]

In any case, theism itself has often toyed with the idea of multiple worlds as a mark of divine creativity. In the history of the early church, Origen argued for multiple universes each with its own drama of creation and salvation. For the standard Christian master-narrative, the creation of the world is preceded by the fall of Satan and other angels from heaven through the misuse of their gifted freedom. At the time of the Renaissance and in the early modern period, several distinguished writers entertained the possibility that there were other worlds remotely located in space. Even Thomas Chalmers, the champion of evangelical theology in the early nineteenth century, entertained thoughts of other worlds and their inhabitants in the renowned *Astronomical Discourses*, lectures delivered in 1815–16 at the Tron Church in Glasgow city centre to packed audiences. So the prospect of other worlds and life forms is probably not one that theology should set its face against too swiftly. In any case, the discovery of intelligent extra-terrestrial life might require the revision of some assumptions particularly with respect to the classical doctrine of redemption. And an openness to its possibility at least militates against an over-wrought anthropocentrism that seeks to exhaust the divine economy by reference to Homo sapiens. The world was not created only for the sake of producing human beings. An eternally creative God may have many other purposes and objects of love. As the closing chapters of Job suggest, the divine wisdom must always outstrip the scope of human comprehension.

When all the smoke has cleared, we seem again to be confronted with the twin questions of why there is a universe at all and why it exhibits a rational structure capable of scientific description by its conscious inhabitants. To these questions, theism offers a single explanation. The new atheists of course are well aware of these arguments. Dawkins tends to dismiss them as cheap dialectical tricks employed by theists, desperate resorts by those who have already yielded to the power of the natural sciences but are too afraid to abandon their religious convictions. Yet these fundamental metaphysical questions remain and are not to be dismissed as either uninteresting or contrived. Why does the world exist at all and why does it exhibit such a complex yet elegant rationality? These are questions of perennial fascination and continue to be raised by physicists and philosophers, many of whom display a sense of wonder that is strangely absent in the writings of the new atheists. Mathematicians sometimes ponder this in aesthetic or religious terms. The Hungarian Nobel Prize winner Eugene Wigner in a famous article in 1960 spoke about the unreasonable effectiveness of mathematics that we neither understand nor deserve.[21] If the modern scientific narrative of cosmology and Darwinian evolution is correct, then we are left as always with the sheer mystery of a world that manifests such complexity and intelligibility.

Two further issues require some comment before venturing a conclusion. The question 'who made God?' is sometimes presented as an effective counter-argument to the claim that the God hypothesis has high explanatory power. Since we cannot explain God, it is said, we should not postulate such an entity to explain the universe. We merely solve one problem at the price of generating another. As a compelling rebuttal this seems to suffer two fundamental weaknesses. First, it is not the case that an explanation of one event should be avoided simply because we cannot offer a full account of the explanation itself. If it functions as the only available candidate to explain the phenomenon, then it ought to be seriously considered. The evidence might for example point to only one person committing a crime. Even if one has no comprehension of motive, this does not make the hypothesis redundant or impossible. Second, philosophers have long argued that an adequate first cause of the universe must be a self-sufficient being, namely one whose existence unlike that of other beings is not dependent upon anything else. This idea of divine aseity is further elucidated by religious convictions about the freedom of God from the conditions and limitations that determine contingent creatures. Divine constancy is closely related to this notion of self-subsistence whereby God cannot be fundamentally altered by created realities. While such a concept of aseity may be the source of much conceptual analysis and contested formulation, as a deep-seated religious conviction it cannot be dismissed in a sentence or two as a theological conjuring trick.

The problem of evil is cited frequently as a telling counter-argument against most forms of theism. Of course, this is highly plausible as a reaction to the standard forms of defence that are offered in the face of both natural and moral evil. Here theologians have typically appealed to the value of free will and also the capacity of evil to elicit greater goods. A condition of freedom and responsibility is that people will make wrong choices with bad consequences for themselves and others. The price of freedom is therefore a measure of evil. Similarly, a process of character development and moral formation will require some experience of hardship, misfortune, and uncertainty in our lives. Without the discipline of pain, we cannot become the persons that God wills us to be. There is something in each of these appeals that contains a measure of validity. Yet they falter, and must appear inadequate and even inappropriate when we are confronted by the sheer scale of evil as in the Shoah, as well as some of its most troubling instances, for example the death of children. And too often suffering does not ennoble us—it destroys instead of refining us. Its magnitude and intensity seem to outweigh decisively any gains that may be afforded.

I do not want to underestimate the gravity of this problem nor the way in which it sometimes leaves people in times of crisis bereft of a faith that they once had. Indeed Charles Darwin may have lost his faith not so much as a result of his science but as the outcome of his intense reaction to the sudden death of his daughter Annie. Nor do I wish to suggest that there is some version of a standard theodicy that will adequately resolve it. As part of a more oblique response, one might instead ask what practical use such a theodicy would have, even if we could discover it. To find an answer to the problem of evil in the big picture, to see its point in the grand scheme and over the long run would not make it much easier to bear or accept suffering in the short and medium terms. At the same time, it would be a mistake to see faith as somehow in denial of the magnitude of evil, as if it were a piece of recalcitrant evidence to which believers had to be deaf or blind. To a significant extent, religion functions as a mechanism for coping with evil and suffering. It does not meet the pain of life as a surd fact that otherwise disrupts a vision of the world that is serene and untroubled. One does not need to delve too deeply into sacred texts to discover this. Themes of struggle and resistance run throughout the Hebrew Bible almost from its opening verses. A cross is the dominant symbol of Christianity. Allah is repeatedly described as merciful. Strategies for coping with evil, grasping its eventual defeat, and dealing with our own complicity are patiently explored. The appropriation of the religious picture or the box of tools described earlier is already engaged with this problem at a practical level.

Again, it needs to be conceded that this is not a simple rejoinder to the sceptic's challenge. Yet it does remind us that the problem is already acknowledged and engaged where faith arises and is practised. For this reason, it is difficult to see the problem of evil as a sudden and successful knock-down argument that can unexpectedly ambush the forces of theism. John Updike, that most theologically driven of recent novelists, hints at this in the closing reflections of one of his later stories. The most solid evidence for the truth of the Christian religion is 'our sensation that something is amiss— that there has been a lapse or slippage in the world and things are not quite as they should be'.[22] Updike's claim is difficult to formulate as a precise argument, but it probably amounts to a rejection of naturalism. Suffering and death are not merely natural phenomena that promote a process of selection and survival. They are experienced as negating the way the world ought to be and by grace how it may eventually become.

Where this discussion leads is to the predictable and rather banal conclusion that there is no available knock-down argument that will finally secure either of the competing positions against its rival. In some ways, this is recognized by exponents on both sides. The project of natural theology today is often that of showing that faith is not unreasonable—it can be held consistently with what we know from philosophy and the natural sciences. It is about 'defeating the defeaters', but no more. It should not seek a deductive proof that will condemn the opposition to incoherence and the admission of defeat. Proof in this sense is simply inappropriate to the nature of the subject matter. On the other side, even a critic like Dennett similarly concedes that the traditional arguments tend to leave one in a state of cognitive suspense. 'I decided some time ago that diminishing returns had set in on the arguments about God's existence, and I doubt that any breakthroughs are in the offing, from either side.'[23]

The differences between faith in God and a naturalist account of the world run too deep and are too wide-ranging to enable a quick and decisive victory for either side. The position we take will inevitably be determined by an extensive cluster of personal, intellectual, and emotional commitments. Although speculative issues cannot be excluded from the range of factors that shape our deepest dispositions, argument is seldom the sole cause of faith or its loss. With its practical dimension, faith requires to be exercised often in the absence of clearly formulated arguments and it may be none the worse for this. The commitment it requires, moreover, may often or always be incommensurate with the measure of understanding and assent we can give to arguments for and against God's existence.

In his recent study *The Secular Age*, Charles Taylor looks at the phenomenon of conversion. Within a climate of considerable hostility and scepticism, faith presents itself not so much as the default position that it was for our ancestors. It is now an 'embattled option'. Converts speak about turning to religion not so much under the compulsion of argument and evidence, but because it provides a set of richer resources for living and understanding the world than is available elsewhere. Many of these converts are artists and writers for whom a sense of the transcendent is otherwise missing. He quotes Flannery O'Connor's remark about 'the conflict between an attraction for the Holy and the disbelief in it that we breathe in the air of our times'.[24] Of course, the introduction of the language of 'conversion' can be quite inflammatory. In a wonderful footnote, Dawkins reports that he has received numerous warnings that he himself is ripe for a deathbed conversion. Many of his correspondents have predicted this, and so irritated is he is by the prospect that he has made provision for a tape-recorder to be switched on at his bedside at the appropriate moment.[25]

The issue of the relationship of faith to reason greatly exercised John Henry Newman in his *University Sermons* and later in the *Grammar of Assent*. Pointing to the practical character of religious belief, he claims that faith is mainly swayed by 'antecedent considerations'. These are its 'previous notices, prepossessions, and (in a good sense of the word) prejudices'.[26] Preaching in 1839 on the text that God has chosen the foolish things of the world to confound the wise, Newman compares the judgements of faith to the wisdom of a great general who 'knows what his friends and enemies are about, and what will be the final result, and where, of their combined movements'. Yet when asked to argue in word or on paper, the same general may find all his conjectures and reasonings to be less than adequate. By analogy, he speaks of

faith (as) a process of reason, in which so much of the grounds of inference cannot be exhibited, so much lies in the character of the mind itself, in its general view of things, its estimate of the probable and the improbable, its impressions concerning God's will, and its anticipations derived from its own inbred wishes, that it will ever seem to the world irrational and despicable—till, that is, the event confirms it.[27]

To the sceptic this will seem rather lame, a case of special pleading at precisely the point where the argument breaks down, a retreat into mere intuition and stubborn persistence of belief when the evidence is to the contrary. In face of this, there are two lines of response. One is to signify that the maintenance of belief does require a posterior rational defence in face of criticism. While its source and practice may not rest upon a carefully reasoned position, nevertheless it requires to offer some counter-argument and defence in face of any sceptical attack. But faith and theoretical reason are not here opposed, merely configured in a particular way. In any case, the intuitive judgement that Newman extols is not confined to religious faith alone, as the analogy with the wise general is intended to show. Intuition characterizes the way we act and react in ethical and artistic matters. Often we get it right or sense something significant without the capacity simultaneously to articulate and defend that judgement. Historians, detectives, and scientists too have their prior commitments, trusted methods, and tacit beliefs all of which inform their work and without which progress in enquiry could not take place.

Religious faith is not really akin to a discussion about whether tooth-fairies, ghosts, or extra-terrestrials exist. We miss the point of faith if we construe it either positively or negatively in those terms. Attention to the nature of cosmological arguments reveals the ways in which God is quite unlike creaturely causes. If God is to suffice as a candidate for the explanation of the world in its totality, then God cannot be a link in a chain of causes. As an agent, God cannot act through the embodied means of hands, arms, legs, or vocal cords. As the primary explanation of all forms of secondary causes, divine causation is not located within any spatio-temporal frame of reference. It was for this reason that Thomas Aquinas reserved the term 'creator' for God, preferring instead to think of creatures as having the capacity only for making. Indeed, Aquinas' arguments for God's existence have been interpreted in recent scholarship not so much as proofs that demonstrate to the sceptic what he or she doubts, but activities of the mind that purify it of the idolatrous assumption that we have a readily accessible knowledge of what is meant by God. These are less exercises in demonstration of God's existence than a directing of the human intellect towards a mysterious limit of thought that in the *Summa Theologiae* can only be further illumined by divine revelation.[28] We move towards but do not reach in the cosmological argument an answer to the question of why there is something rather than nothing, of wherein lies the origin of all that we experience.[29]

The contingency of the world has often been a source of wonder to philosophers and cosmologists whether aesthetic, religious, or intellectual in form. Yet the contingency that marks the evolutionary story has been the source more often of doubt to biologists and others. The seemingly haphazard routes taken by life on earth, the intersection of different causal sequences and the prevalence of extinction, waste, and suffering seem to tell a different story from that of fine-tuning and cosmic coincidences. In the following chapter, we shall explore the scope of neo-Darwinism in relation to the history of life on earth, and ask whether its explanatory power can extend even to religious belief and activity.

Notes

1. Richard Dawkins, *The God Delusion* (London: Bantam, 2006), 52.
2. Ludwig Wittgenstein, *Lectures and Conversations on Aesthetics, Psychology and Religious Belief* (Oxford: Blackwell, 1966), 56.
3. What needs to be added to this further remark of Wittgenstein is that there may be many people for whom something in between these options is the norm.
4. *The God Delusion*, 14.
5. John Brooke and Geoffrey Cantor, *Reconstructing Nature: The Engagement of Science and Religion* (Edinburgh: T&T Clark, 1998), 143ff.
6. M. A. Stewart, 'Religion and Rational Theology', in Alexander Broadie (ed.), *The Cambridge Companion to the Scottish Enlightenment* (Cambridge: Cambridge University Press, 2003), 31–59 at 37.
7. This is the central thesis of *Rocks of Ages: Science and Religion in the Fullness of Life* (London, Jonathan Cape, 2001).
8. Ibid., 59.
9. Ibid., 65.

10. Richard Swinburne, *The Existence of God* (Oxford: Clarendon Press, 1979).
11. I have sought to deal with this in *The Cosmos and the Creator* (London: SPCK, 1998) 49ff. See also Kenneth Miller, *Finding Darwin's God: A Scientist's Search for Common Ground between God and Evolution* (Harper: New York, 1999).
12. See Paul Copan and William Lane Craig, *Creation out of Nothing: A Biblical, Philosophical and Scientific Exploration* (Grand Rapids, MI: Baker, 2004), 219ff.
13. Martin Rees, *Just Six Numbers: The Deep Forces that Shape the Universe* (London: Weidenfeld & Nicolson, 1999).
14. Here I am following the discussion in Rodney D. Holder, *God, the Multiverse and Everything* (Aldershot: Ashgate, 2004), 50ff.
15. Martin Rees, *Just Six Numbers*, 173.
16. Martin Rees, 'Other Universes: A Scientific Perspective', in Neil Manson (ed.), *God and Design: The Teleological Argument and Modern Science* (London: Routledge, 2003), 211–20.
17. Robin Collins, 'Multiverse hypothesis: a theistic perspective', in Bernard Carr (ed.), *Universe or Multiverse* (Cambridge: Cambridge University Press, 2007), 459–80 at 466.
18. Paul Davies, *The Goldilocks Enigma: Why is the Universe just Right for Life?* (Harmondsworth: Penguin, 2007).
19. This is argued by George Ellis, 'Multiverses: description, uniqueness and testing', in Bernard Carr (ed.), *Universe or Multiverse*, 387–410 at 394.
20. This is discussed by Neil Manson, *God and Design: The Teleological Argument and Modern Science* (London: Routledge, 2003), 18ff.
21. 'The Unreasonable Effectiveness of Mathematics in the Natural Sciences', *Communications in Pure and Applied Mathematics*, 13.1 (1960), 1–14.
22. John Updike, *Villages* (London: Penguin, 2006), 312.
23. Daniel C. Dennett, *Breaking the Spell: Religion as a Natural Phenomenon* (London: Penguin, 2007), 27.
24. Charles Taylor, *The Secular Age* (Cambridge, MA: Harvard University Press, 2007), 732.
25. *The God Delusion*, 98.
26. John Henry Newman, *University Sermons* (London: SPCK, 1970), 187.
27. Ibid., 217–18.

28. See Fergus Kerr's discussion in *After Aquinas: Versions of Thomism* (Oxford: Blackwell, 2002). For a recent discussion of the role of the *via negativa* in Aquinas see Kevin Hector, 'Apophaticism in Thomas Aquinas: A Reformulation and Recommendation', *Scottish Journal of Theology*, 60 (2007), 377–93.
29. See Herbert McCabe, *God Matters* (London: Chapman, 1987), 6.

3

DARWINISM: HOW MUCH DOES IT EXPLAIN?

The Compatibility of Design and Evolution

A curious feature of recent writing on the science–theology interface is the different direction in which arguments from contingency move. In the previous chapter, we noticed one movement from evidence of particularity to inference of design. The physical universe as we can observe and describe it has a particular form and content. It is governed by specific physical constants, including the four fundamental forces of nature, that enable the emergence of stars, planets, and carbon-based life forms over a period of time spanning many billions of years. Our increasing awareness of this structure has led to the rehabilitation of the design argument with its focus on fine-tuning, cosmic coincidences, and the strong anthropic principle. The fact that our universe appears as a one-off and could have been so different is adduced as reason for assuming that it has been intended by a divine agency. This is illustrated by Freeman Dyson's oft-quoted remark, 'The more I examine the Universe and examine the details of its architecture, the more evidence I find that the Universe in some sense must have known we were coming.'[1]

Where the evolution of life is concerned, however, the story of contingency can lead to the very opposite conclusion. The particular course of evolutionary history as revealed by palaeobiology suggests randomness, waste, and an absence of direction and therefore purpose. Punctuated by mass extinctions, the story of life on earth over hundreds of millions of years seems not to lead anywhere but to represent a haphazard burgeoning of myriad life forms followed by their demise and succession by others. Having held to a traditional form of the design argument in his early life, Charles Darwin appears gradually to have abandoned his faith. Historians debate whether this was on account of his grief following the death of his ten-year-old daughter Annie in 1851 or a consequence of his gradual discovery of the mechanisms of evolution. Whether such biographical features can ever be entirely separated is doubtful. At any rate, the crisis of Annie's death seems to have led to the further diminution of his belief in divine providence. His favourite child, Annie was a source of much love and affection to her father. Her death, probably as a result of scarlet fever, confirmed his abiding sense of sickness and mortality. He is reported as having been shocked by 'the dreadful but quiet war of organic beings' amidst what appeared to be 'peaceful woods and smiling fields'.[2] Darwin's case illustrates the fusion of personal and intellectual factors in one's faith position, and indeed raises the question of whether one's beliefs can ever reach a stasis or become altogether free of incoherence. Towards the end of his life, he confessed in a letter to his friend Joseph Hooker, 'My theology is a simple muddle.'[3] He was not alone in that respect.

The contingent status of the phenomena has thus tended to strike scientific observers in two ways. One move, as we have seen, is from cosmic origins towards the conclusion of design. Fine-tuning suggests that our emergence was determined already in the first milliseconds of the universe's history. The other is from the apparent accident of anthropological evolution to a metaphysical naturalism whether agnostic or outwardly atheist. The lack of any rhyme or reason in the story of life on earth suggests that it is an evolutionary accident, one that can be explained scientifically but not such as to suggest, let alone demand, explanation in terms of an overarching intentionality. However, upon qualification these claims may not be as starkly oppositional as first appears.[4]

The most familiar example of the claim for radical contingency is Stephen Jay Gould's conviction that the course of evolution has a probability not unlike that of a National Lottery rollover. The vast majority of life forms found in the Burgess Shale—fossil records in British Columbia from 500 million years ago—have no modern representatives. The survival of a only a handful of phyla is itself the result of contingent forces, by which is meant intersecting causal sequences in the environment. At the end of the Permian period around 96 per cent of marine species disappeared, and during the Cretaceous period most of the dinosaurs suffered extinction. These may have been the results of sudden environmental changes that impacted evolutionary history from the outside, as it were. This leads Gould to conclude that the tape of life even if run a million times over from its starting point would not yield anything like Homo sapiens again. However, other neo-Darwinists have been less persuaded by this radical contingency thesis. The struggle for survival will tend to select some physical and intellectual attributes, even if it is a process with unpredictable twists and outcomes. So, for some, the appearance of mammals with large brains is not as improbable as Gould suggests.

This thesis has been taken further in the recent work of Simon Conway Morris, who himself worked on the Burgess Shale. For Conway Morris, there are always constraints on the evolutionary process and patterns of convergence that can be detected. Taking the analogy of the discovery of Easter Island by the Polynesians hundreds of years ago, he argues that

although this seems improbable given its miniature size amidst
the vastness of the Pacific Ocean, in other ways an inevitability
attaches to it. When one considers the adventurous travels
of the Polynesian peoples, their navigation skills, the design
of their vessels and so forth, the discovery of Easter Island
becomes highly probable even if the precise time and the
successful crew cannot be predicted. So it is with the story
of evolution. A series of constraints acts upon the trajectories
that life forms can take with the result that mammals with
DNA, camera eyes, enlarged brains, tools, and technology are
likely to appear. This is evolutionary constraint rather than
determinism: not every detail is predictable or guaranteed yet
a pattern is discernible.

The haunting subtitle of Conway Morris's book *Life's Solution* is 'Inevitable Humans in a Lonely Universe'. The point
he urges is that the planetary conditions for animal evolution
are likely to be highly rare in the cosmos. The earth needs to
be the right size and at the right distance from its sun. It needs
the protection from meteoroids of other, denser planets in
the solar system, since these would arrest evolutionary history
were they to strike the surface of our planet too frequently.
The precise odds here are somewhat speculative and in any
case a theory of theistic evolution does not require the claim
that there is no intelligent extra-terrestrial life. Nevertheless, Conway Morris's striking work has the merit of showing
against Gould that, if run again, the tape of life might display
not an identical pattern but a fair degree of similarity with what
has happened already. Evolution is not just a random walk.
This leads towards the further conclusion that even if there
is intelligent life on other planets, and Conway Morris is less
confident about this than many, it will not be as unlike our
forms of life as some science fiction suggests. Quoting Robert
Bieri, he writes, 'If we ever succeed in communicating with
conceptualising beings in outer space, they won't be spheres,

pyramids, cubes or pancakes. In all probability they will look an awful lot like us.'[5]

Despite his commendable caution around wider metaphysical issues, Conway Morris is clearly sketching an account of evolutionary history that is consonant with theistic design. He argues against sheer contingency in favour of convergence, constraint, and general evolutionary direction. The plot is not predictable, but in retrospect we can see that increasing complexity in a humanoid direction is inevitable. This gives his evolutionary science a rather different philosophical slant from other Darwinian accounts. Nevertheless, he sharply distinguishes his position from creation science and intelligent design (ID) theory neither of which he entertains seriously. Both suffer from a confusion of religious and scientific explanation, although ID theory is more subtle and has had some notable exponents since its appearance in the 1990s. Its emergence might be dated from Philip Johnson's attack on Darwinism, which sought to punch holes in its case around issues such as the origin of life, the explanatory power of natural selection, and gaps in the fossil record. This was followed soon after by Michael Behe's much discussed book, *Darwin's Black Box* (1996), which seemed to provide a scientific complement to Johnson's scepticism.[6]

Behe's leading claim is that organic life forms display instances of self-organized complexity that cannot be explained on neo-Darwinian, incremental terms. His most famous example is of the bacterial flagellum, a kind of outboard motor that enables the bacterium to move efficiently and thus to survive and replicate. According to Behe, this feature of the bacterium cannot have evolved in stages. It is a complex system of interlocking parts, any one of which if slightly mutated would cause the whole to break down. It is simply not possible, therefore, to account for its emergence on neo-Darwinian principles of explanation. Some other mechanism must be required and the only available candidate appears to be an intentional process of design that causes this and similar instances of organized complexity. Behe's work has been conceptually reinforced by William Dembski's discussion of the differences between design and chance. The former exhibits the properties of contingency, complexity, and specification. Where these appear to be satisfied in the case of organized complexity we are entitled to assume that we are witnessing the effects of design.

The hypothesis of intelligent design is dependent upon the breakdown of Darwinian principles at key points. Its explanatory function is not denied, as in creation science, but merely regarded as insufficient. There is no commitment to a young earth or resistance to the idea that species may have emerged and diversified from a common source through a long process of descent. In arguing that Darwinism is consistent with design, the ID theorists are on to something. But the strategy of seeking to close down the power of Darwinian explanation within the domain of biology is deeply problematic for reasons that are methodological, scientific, and theological. First, as a methodology it seeks to make an informed contribution to physical explanation by refusing to bracket out divine agency. Yet as science, it has not contributed to new research programmes, been confirmed by its predictive power, or yielded unexpected discoveries. All of these might have been expected were this to represent a significant advance on previous scientific understanding. A survey of research databases until 2001 found that amidst hundreds of thousands of publications, only a tiny fraction referred to ID as a biological theory and none of these could report research based on the theory.[7] A second issue concerns its scientific claims. The argument moves from a perceived failure or absence of natural physical principles of explanation to the postulation of a design mechanism. Yet this is highly redolent of a God-of-the-gaps procedure. Let's find what science has been unable to explain and then postulate God, it seems to propose. Behe would contest this by arguing that he has shown that the bacterial flagellum is constructed in such a way that prevents Darwinian explanation. It is not merely a gap but the very nature of the phenomenon that compels an account in terms of design. However, this is to give hostages to fortune. What if science produces an explanation along Darwinian lines that we were unaware of and could not envisage in the early 1990s? The ID theory then collapses. This indeed appears to be pretty much what is happening in the case of the bacterial flagellum—Francis Collins, evangelical Christian and director of the human genome project in the USA, describes it as 'the poster child of ID'.[8] Several components of the bacteria now appear to be related to a different apparatus for attacking other bacteria. This 'type III secretory apparatus' enables the survival of the organisms that possess it. By being adapted along with other proteins for a new use, it is possible that the motor was generated incrementally. This is a research programme in progress but it is a genuine one that avoids a lazy and hazardous appeal to design. As science, therefore, ID theory yields too many hostages and it seems already to be paying the price.

From a theological perspective, moreover, there are at least two besetting problems with ID theory. One is to specify exactly how, where, and when an intelligent agent conditions the evolutionary process. Where is the causal joint and how can we inspect it? At what point and in what way does God assemble the bacterial flagellum? If ID theory is to stand as science then it needs to offer some account of divine action that can be included in a scientific textbook. Here, it seems to me, ID theorists have little to say. More importantly, the need for a divine designer to intervene at various junctures in the history of evolution also suggests a defect in the original plan. A creation endowed with a fruitfulness that will bring forth increasingly complex life forms is one that may betoken evidence of design. But it is important to recognize that it does so in terms of its original integrity. From the outset, it is fit for purpose. Indeed this seems more consistent with the cosmology of Genesis and the early church, which deems the good creation to have been fully endowed by its Maker from the beginning.

In this context, Howard van Til speaks of the 'formational economy of the universe'. This is 'the set of all of the dynamic capabilities of matter and material, physical and biotic systems that contribute to the actualization of both inanimate structures and biotic forms in the course of the universe's formational history'.[9] He argues that in its robust form this principle claims that the universe possesses all the necessary properties to make possible over the course of time the process of macroevolution. While this is a presupposition of scientific investigation, it is also viewed with suspicion by many Christian apologists as leading to a metaphysical naturalism that excludes most forms of religious explanation. To some degree, this suspicion is fuelled by secular critics of religion who tend to argue that the absence of divine intervention in natural processes renders religious explanation redundant. In his striking metaphor of cranes and skyhooks, Dennett writes about the ways in which the skyhooks have gradually disappeared as science finds more cranes to do the work. A skyhook is of course an analogue for a supernatural intelligence that intervenes to bring about important changes in evolutionary history that would not otherwise occur. The crane is an earthbound mechanism that enables lifting and movement in incremental stages.

For over a century, skeptics have been trying to find a proof that Darwin's idea just can't work, at least *not all the way*. They have been hoping for, hunting for, praying for skyhooks, as exceptions to what they see as the bleak vision of Darwin's algorithm churning away. And time and again, they have come by with truly interesting challenges—leaps and gaps and other marvels that do so seem, at first, to need skyhooks. But then along have come the cranes, discovered in many cases by the very skeptics who were hoping to find a skyhook.[10]

But, in setting the terms of the debate in this way, both sides ignore the possibility of complementary forms of description. A theory of theistic evolution does not depend upon exploiting gaps in the capacity of science to explain how later stages of natural history emerge from earlier ones. It is a characterization of the whole process, one that is originally and inherently endowed with a capacity for macroevolution. To put the point more cautiously, there is nothing to prevent the theist from claiming that divine agency resides, not in particular adjustments to the flow of evolution, but in creating and sustaining a cosmos that is informed with sufficient natural properties to bring this about.

One might see the mistake of ID theory in terms of transferring from general providence to special providence the endowment of the creation with the properties that are necessary for an evolving world. Of course, there is no *a priori* reason why a Creator might not make the world through occasional adjustments to its order, but as far as I can tell it adds nothing either to divine providence or to the grandeur of the world to assume this. And given the aforementioned methodological and scientific problems that ID theory encounters, it seems unwise to claim divine design merely on account of a perceived inadequacy in current scientific explanation. To quote Collins again, 'this ship is not headed to the promised land; it is headed instead to the bottom of the ocean'.[11]

The complementarity of different types of description is central to the argument that is being advanced here. No one discipline or perspective can tell the whole story. Types of description include the scientific and the religious, but the list is not exhaustive. Against the attempt of any one discipline to exclude in principle another, I am arguing for multiple levels or dimensions of description. Even when we cannot offer an adequate account of how these co-inhere, it seems unnecessarily reductive to privilege one type of explanation over every other. This is the flaw in both the secularism of the new atheists, who assume that the extension of scientific explanation must render design otiose, and their religious opponents who seek to deny the power of evolutionary science and modern cosmology. What is required is a greater degree of intellectual humility which recognises that many forms of description are required to account for the complexity of the world and human life. Of course, this does not amount to handing out blank cheques to everyone who claims to represent a form of enquiry different from one's own. But it does take a willingness to admit that there is no single vantage point—an Archimedean perspective—that will privilege one type of explanation over every other. Emmanuel Levinas, the Jewish philosopher, writes about the dangers of a 'totalising' view that seeks to vanquish every other type of account and to insist uniquely upon its own universe of discourse. Elsewhere, John Polkinghorne has given the more mundane example of describing what is going on when one makes a cup of tea. It involves physics to describe the movement of one's body and the force of electricity, chemistry to account for the boiling of water and the infusion of the tea, and biology to understand our capacity to drink and digest. Nevertheless, these powerful scientific explanations do not exclude also a personal account of what is happening—reasons as well as causes. A friend has called to whom I have offered a cup of tea as a gesture of hospitality. To describe this one might want to include anthropological, social-scientific, and ethical categories. His point is that a privileging of any one of these types of description would diminish our understanding of what is happening.

Evolutionary Psychology and Religion

With this in mind, we turn now to the most important scientific development in the recent study of religion. While it is appealed to by recent critics, it engages a much wider cross-disciplinary body of scholars. This is the application of evolutionary psychology or cognitive science to the phenomenon of religion.[12]

In the past, Marx attempted to explain religion on the basis of economic forces and Freud on psychological grounds, but today's theorists tend to occupy the terrain of neo-Darwinism. Our religious behaviour is to be accounted for in terms of a range of ancestral habits, all of which are closely related to survival strategies, and which predispose us towards religious belief and practice. Rather than seeing religion as a unique and *sui generis* subject requiring a peculiar set of explanations, evolutionary psychology situates it within its broader account of the human brain and the capacities and dispositions that it has evolved. The mind is not so much a *tabula rasa*, a blank slate awaiting the conditioning of nurture and upbringing by parents, teachers, and others. As one recent commentator puts it, 'Instead, the human mind comes factory-equipped with an astonishing array of dedicated psychological mechanisms, designed over deep time by natural and sexual selection, to solve the hundreds of statistically recurring adaptive problems that our ancestors confronted. Understanding those mechanisms of mind requires understanding their evolved functions—what they were designed by selection to accomplish.'[13]

In Dawkins and Dennett there is an acknowledged borrowing from the work of several scholars who have sought to apply the methods of evolutionary psychology to religion. The arguments are well summarized by Dennett, following Pascal Boyer's argument in his book *Religion Explained*.[14]

The basic strategy is to see how several gadgets or tools that the human brain evolves combine in creative ways to produce the beliefs and practices that typically shape religion. These tools include what is called the intentional stance, a hyper-active detection agency, various alarm systems, detectors, generators, and a yearning for stories. It is not possible to do justice to the complexity of these accounts. What follows is only a flavour of what is proposed.

First, what is called 'the intentional stance' has proved important to the survival of species. By attributing intentions, beliefs, and desires to things in our environment we anticipate predators and so evade them. This is evident from our study of animal behaviour. Second, the ability to include counter-intuitive information that cuts across normal categories of classification is a pervasive feature of human life. It is useful to us in understanding and behaving successfully in the world. Experiments with children show how well adapted they are for this sort of activity. They can imagine objects as animate and animals as personal, possessing characteristics and behaving in ways that transcend their normal categories. This capacity to absorb counter-intuitive information is evident in the case of religious concepts. Cutting across standard conceptual boundaries, these describe persons without a body, natural objects with a physiology, plants with animate powers, and tools with cognition.[15]

Closely linked to this is a hyper-active agent detection device (HADD) by which we attribute too much intentionality to our environment. For example, your dog will often bark at unfamiliar sounds around the house such as snow falling off the roof, even when such sounds have not been caused by another agent.[16] This is part of the dog's finely tuned survival mechanism and in non-domesticated animals it is even more apparent. In human culture, our intentional stances are exhibited in the use of language to imagine and anticipate the world as populated by other agents with similar intentions to ourselves. Indeed, as research confirms, to lack this capacity to represent other people's representations (as in autism) is to be significantly disadvantaged. With the power of language we tend to use this hyper-active intentional stance to fantasize. We populate the world with spirits, fairies, mythical creatures, and fabulous monsters who in different ways give expression to our wishes and fears. This is an important source of superstition whereby we assume that natural processes are under the causal influence of invisible and unknown agencies. As Atran summarizes, 'Supernatural agents arise by cultural manipulation of stimuli in the natural domain of folk psychology, which evolved trip-wired to detect animate agents.'[17]

But why do we do this? Here evolutionary psychology does not rest with a simple explanation in terms of the reasons that people typically offer for holding their beliefs. In general, these would be adjudged unpersuasive as well as lacking in proper explanatory power. A deeper account requires us to look at our mental basement, as it were. What goes on beneath the conscious processes of reasoning is needed to explain our natural tendency to think and act in the ways we do. In this context, an account is offered in terms of the importance of securing access to the right strategic information. It works along the following lines.

There is an obvious survival advantage in having reliable information passed on to you by your parents about how your environment works. So we tend to believe what fathers, mothers, and elders tell us, since this keeps us safe and moving along the straight and narrow. Without this dependency, which is normally reliable, our prospects in life would be severely diminished. Much of what we need to know in order to survive is received by a process of cultural transmission. This generates attitudes of trust in the reliability of certain types of person, most notably our parents and teachers. From this natural propensity to ascribe information and control to others, there arises a further tendency to project onto our dead ancestors or the gods a capacity to possess strategic information that if acquired would enhance our own prospects. We know that the remembering of the dead, as personal information systems, is maintained through the burial customs of Homo sapiens. These ideal persons are described by Boyer as 'full-access strategic agents'.[18] However, if inaccessible this information is of little use to us, so we need to identify ways of divining it and securing access to what otherwise lies beyond us. This works through divination by ritual, usually involving a shaman or holy person. Thus a religious caste emerges that perpetuates itself by retaining exclusive access to important information, for example about the healing properties of particular herbs or practices. This relieves us of the stress of having to work out these things for ourselves and so affords reassurance while also releasing energies for other tasks. We see modern analogues to these aspects of ancient folk religion in the effects of hypnotism and placebo-effect medical treatment, something of which scientists have been aware for a long time. In all this, we have evolving folk religious practices that in turn are transformed into the organized religions with which we are now more familiar.

There are at least two further phases of the explanatory account, as we proceed from folk religions to the more institutionalized and prevalent world religions. The first appeals to the advantages to the members of a group in having an organized and elaborate religion. It creates moral and social cohesion that will reinforce the identity, security, and even prosperity of the group. After all, there has been no shortage of sermons on the social benefits of sound morality and decent God-fearing habits. Religion turns 'otherwise hapless populations of unrelated and mutually suspicious people into tightly knit families or even highly effective super-organisms, rather like ant colonies or beehives'.[19]

According to Dennett, this phenomenon is itself not sufficient to explain its emergence. We also need a secondary account of how standard theistic beliefs, e.g. the omniscience and omnipresence of God, can take a hold within groups. Here he reverts to the further explanatory device of memes as cultural replicators. Religion spreads and takes a hold in a way that is largely subliminal and sub-rational. This further turn in the argument sends the explanatory theory downwards into biological and mimetic drives. Rather likes a virus, the meme enables or represents the spread of an idea in different ways throughout a population. Only a very small number of memes are selected but these can become powerfully embedded in religious institutions.

A development of this naturalistic story might appeal to the economics of religion. According to one approach, in modern democratic and capitalist societies we witness an evolution of religion into competing products from which consumers select according to their needs, interests, and desires. (This feature of rational choice distinguishes our group behaviour from insect behaviour, for example.) So in America and to a lesser extent in Europe, we have people shopping around to buy into the most potent religious product on offer, one that will enhance their prospects of survival and prosperity. This is why, according to the analysis, evangelicalism with its stronger claims is also likely to outperform more moderate forms of Christianity in today's religious supermarket.

So here we have the rudiments of a contemporary natural-istic explanation. Religion has its roots in ancestral behaviour that, from a rational perspective, is essentially a misfiring of deep survival strategies. This disposes us towards the belief that the world is ruled by supernatural agencies which can be accessed and in part controlled by the rituals, beliefs, and institutions of religions. The prevalence of religion together with its typical manifestations can thus be explained. It is only fair to note that Dennett himself recognizes that this is highly speculative, its details being in need of serious scientific research. But its rootedness in biological evolution together with a number of studies already undertaken suggests that it is a promising line of enquiry. What is its status and significance? So far few philosophers of religion or theologians have engaged with this material, but they will certainly need to do so in the future. The following comments are ventured as an initial theological response.

By its own admission this theory is underdetermined by the evidence. The resources from pre-literate societies are quite sparse and elusive by comparison with the recent documented history of organized religion. The research programmes in this field are still at an early stage. Dennett claims that these hypotheses are potentially fruitful but that it will take several decades of research to establish anything like them.[20] However, given a broad evolutionary perspective, it seems reasonable to assume that a phenomenon as old, universal, and varied as religion must be explained at least in part by our evolutionary drives and the advantage that religion conferred upon societies and their members. Moreover, as Boyer and others point out, elements of the theory can be isolated experimentally leading to results with some explanatory power and predictive value. These elements cohere with the picture that is gradually emerging of other cognitive processes, particularly in child development, that show the significance of patterns of brain activation for the standard ways in which we think and behave. Phenomena surrounding language, face recognition, and the transmission of stories can all be illuminated by this line of enquiry. Once we discover the importance of patterns of cerebral activity that have evolved over millions of years for the ways we perceive and inhabit the world, then it is highly likely that these must be part of the story of why human beings seem incorrigibly religious. Grounded in well-established scientific practice, this research programme promises to be more durable than the more speculative explanations of religious belief and behaviour offered by Feuerbach, Marx, and Freud.

The appeal to a mental basement, largely determined by the way the brain has evolved, can be illustrated by the analogy of going to a restaurant for a meal, something that we think we readily understand and imagine. We think of the tables, chairs, and cutlery, the menus placed before us, the staff who serve us, and the food and drink as they are presented and consumed before the bill is paid and the gratuity offered. Yet this is only part of the story. There is the supply of materials to the restaurant, the cooking that goes on usually behind closed doors, the much larger complement of staff required to produce the food, perhaps the most important of whom we never see. Only recently, through reality TV and the expletives of Gordon Ramsay, have we begun to achieve a fuller comprehension of what is involved in the process of dining out. So also with the mind—the reasons that we typically adduce for believing and acting in the ways we do are only a part of the total explanation required. Behind this there are structures, processes, and deep ancestral habits that have emerged through long years of physical evolution. Given our increasing awareness of the contribution made by the evolution of the human brain to language acquisition *inter alia*, it would be surprising if this did not have a contribution to make to our understanding of the origins of religion—a pervasive feature of culture everywhere.

In some measure, evolutionary psychology must account for much that is compelling and pervasive in religion. For instance, it can explain why the most reliable factor in predicting your religious orientation is that of your parents. One does not need to adhere to a doctrine of infant baptism to recognize the importance of parental nurture in religion. It might also suggest why those forms of faith that stress the control exercised over natural processes by the divine are most likely to be successful. The less the gods do for us, the less we are likely to worship or pay attention to them. Research has shown that those who believe ardently in extra-terrestrial visitations do not think and act in ways that are typically religious.[21] The explanation for this seems to be that these extra-terrestrials, despite their technological accomplishments, do not have access to information and exercise influence over what happens to us in our daily lives. Hence, a religion that promises much in terms of access to truly strategic agents is more likely to command our total allegiance. Boyer also extends this argument to make the claim that easier and quicker access to the information offered by religious authorities is always likely to prevail against scientific explanation. This might account for the widespread scepticism surrounding evolutionary theory itself in sectors of Christianity and Islam. It may also help to explain why those religions that offer exclusive knowledge and benefits in an uncertain world are likely to be more successful in the supermarket of faiths. By contrast, more ecumenical, open, and modest approaches may struggle for consumer appeal.

However, one paradoxical feature of all this is that it suggests that religion is very unlikely to disappear under the conditions of modernity. If evolutionary psychology tells us that we are programmed to be religious, then the secularization thesis cannot be true. The pervasiveness of religion is noted by Boyer in his concluding chapter and also by Scott Atran.[22] This, however, creates some dissonance since many leading exponents of evolutionary explanation think of religions as false in all the distinctive claims that they make. The selection of seemingly bizarre examples of belief and practice betoken this, as well as the trend towards downwards explanation. Once the theorist has done his or her work, then there is little else to be explained. The story told is intended, it seems, to give a scientific explanation that will confirm *inter alia* that our religious beliefs are manifestly false. I do not think that it is unfair to detect this as an axiom of much enquiry, although not every cognitive scientist of course adopts this position. Todd Tremlin in his overview of the cognitive foundations of religion says that we are dealing here with a story of origins. It has nothing to do the truthfulness or otherwise of particular religious claims. Yet, many exponents of this burgeoning discipline seem committed to more totalitarian claims. The projectionist subtitle of Boyer's book makes this abundantly clear—'the human instincts that *fashion* gods, spirits and ancestors' (italics mine). What emerges here is a particular form of intellectual elitism. Religion is another evolutionary spandrel—a side consequence of our structural complexity that gives rise to beliefs that are rationally untenable and practices that we can well do without. Hence, we have a caste of theorists who can understand that religion is clearly false and who can also explain why the benighted majority will continue to believe and practice. And yet the same theory seems to predict that even when vindicated those adhering to it will always be in a small minority. This may not be incoherent but it does seem to contain a paradoxical element. Here is an intellectual, professorial elite which alone understands religion and which stands apart from the benighted masses who continue to practise it.[23] We have been here before. The privileged vantage point of cognitive science enables a few to see what is really going on, as opposed to what appears to be happening to the practitioners themselves.

One might legitimately argue that this account of the evolutionary origins of religion does not in itself pronounce on the truth value of belief in God. We could view the disposition towards belief in God as natural and intuitive without supposing that this commits us to theological scepticism. An analogy with common perceptual beliefs might illustrate this quite well. Our cognitive equipment enables us to acquire largely through intuition a useful stock of true beliefs in other areas. We come naturally to a host of beliefs about our world and other people. Evolutionary psychology has a good story to tell here. Yet this is entirely compatible with a reflective commitment to the truthfulness of these beliefs. Origin and truth-value may thus be coincidental insofar as our evolutionary programming furnishes us with what turn out to be justified true beliefs. A similar story along the following lines might be attempted with reference to religious belief. We are well equipped by the evolution of our brains and the circumstances of our environment to believe in God. The durability and extent of monotheism seems to attest the embeddedness of belief in God. Although it is not inevitable or ineradicable, our natural circumstances incline us towards it. A belief in God may therefore turn out to be both natural and well-founded. In this respect, one might attempt to see evolutionary psychology and theology as more-or-less compatible.[24] Theologians, such as Calvin, have insisted that the *sensus divinitatis* is natural to human beings. Perhaps this is now being corroborated by the work of cognitive psychology.

Yet for many of its most zealous exponents, evolutionary psychology seems to render any such discussion otiose. The point of religion has already been explained in psychological terms; there is no need to invoke a transcendental explanation. This would be beside that point. What we have here, in Plantinga's terms, is a *de jure* account of religion that renders all the *de facto* arguments redundant.[25] It is not so much that we are driven to religion by what makes it true, as in the case of perceptual belief. Instead our coming to believe is to be explained not rationally but psychologically. While these might be construed as compatible, this does not appear to be the intention of those expounding the explanation with such evangelical fervour. Beliefs, which seem intuitively false to the theorist, are adequately accounted for in terms of our evolutionary drives and habits. There is little left but for the religionist to recognize this and to find ways of bowing to the inevitable. Yet, as Plantinga also shows, much of the *de jure* case presupposes already that *de facto* arguments for religion are false. Since they are false, our beliefs in God must be explained by an error-theory about their origins and persistence. But in this respect the *de jure* case simply begs the question if the *de facto* case has not been properly investigated and discussed. In much of the literature on religion and cognition, it is difficult to avoid the impression of such question-begging on the *de facto* case. If instead we arrive at a different position on the *de facto* case for God, then the *de jure* argument must fall in seeking to 'explain away' religion even if it remains as an account of the natural conditions surrounding the origin of such beliefs.

Whether Boyer himself considers the best rejoinders to his own position is at least an open question. He argues very swiftly that religion and science are on a collision course and that there will be only one winner. In doing so, he quickly dismisses a more sophisticated approach that he attributes to recent scientists. The attempt to purify religion of inconvenient superstition by positing a kind of deism is dismissed as akin to marketing a car without an engine.[26] He then notes that in practical contexts people have had religious thoughts that do some useful work. Yet this is left unexplored and unrelated to his trite dismissal of a purified religion. We have already seen a peremptory discarding of more practical, chastened, and reflective forms of religious faith in Dawkins. Here again, the critic prefers to treat softer targets as paradigmatic, leaving aside the harder, more reflective cases as somehow not really relevant, interesting, or valid.

However, important attempts to reflect critically upon more superstitious, naïve, and self-serving forms of religion are already well under way in the ancient canonical traditions of the world religions. There we find processes of self-criticism and reflection taking place long before the advent of modern science and deism. Take, for example, the Book of Job, composed in the ancient near east around the sixth century BCE. It inspects and rejects a range of typical claims about the correlation between human virtue and suffering. The ways of God are often beyond us and require a discipline of intellectual humility

and self-correction. Easy correlations between faithful practice and material rewards are dismissed. Simplistic notions of
divine intervention in worldly affairs are queried. The myste-
riousness of God and the limitations of human knowledge are
stressed, not so much under the impact of external challenge
but from within the reflexive act of faith itself.

In seeking to explain the pervasiveness of the world religions, Dennett tends to appeal to the highly controversial
notion of the meme. A term coined by Dawkins, it is intended
to parallel in the cultural domain some function of the 'gene' at
the biological levels. Just as genes are replicated in phenotypes,
so memes spread like contagion amidst human cultures. They
are described as a 'virus of the mind' that spreads in subliminal and non-rational ways. The concept is made to do much
explanatory work, but how successful is this? Some scientists,
such as Conway Morris, dispute whether it explains anything
that cannot be accounted for in different ways by a range
of disciplines.[27] Others have asked awkward questions about
what exactly a meme is in terms of brain functions.[28] It has
not been experimentally detected and isolated in the way in
which genes have clearly been. A further important difficulty
is that it does not appear to allow sufficient scope for the
critical inspection, discrimination, and teaching of ideas. This
is what happens in human cultures and the survival of ideas is
at least partially dependent on a process of rational criticism
and evaluation. Presumably scientific theory and atheism are
themselves memes, according to Dawkins and Dennett, yet
these are still held to be capable of rational vindication as
opposed merely to a virus-like process of transmission.

Furthermore, the extent to which cognitive science can adequately explain religion is questioned by many social scientists.
Once we reach the specifics of human behaviour, culture, and
religion, then other explanatory and descriptive mechanisms
come into play. The cognitive approach tends to think of
religions in terms of a set of beliefs and rituals concerning

supernatural agents such as gods, ghosts, demons, and fairies. But whether this rather narrow and essentialist account can capture the extent to which faith involves a wide-ranging set of practices, commitments, and dispositions is doubtful. Religion is not to be treated as a compartment of our cognitive stock so much as a way of living in the world. It involves practical skills, ethical valuation, artistic expression, and the kind of assessment that philosophers and theologians in different traditions have sought to develop. Cognitive science may offer something useful in describing why human beings are disposed to believe in the supernatural and how we come to be incorrigibly superstitious. But in dealing with the emergence of relatively long and self-reflective religious traditions a broader set of descriptive tools and evaluative concepts will be required.

This anxiety about a narrowness of approach relates to a broader concern that the human person is too readily identified as an information processing system determined by its genetic drives. By dealing only with the hard-wiring of the brain, we are in danger of neglecting how its capacities are differently expressed in processes of development and social organization. Tim Ingold speaks about our being 'soft assembled' rather than 'hard wired'.[29] It is the dynamic and complex patterns of social life and practice that make us what we are. The richness of these cannot be accounted for entirely by genetic drives and cognitive dispositions. Explaining why we believe x, y, and z in terms of malformed adaptive strategies does not really begin to deal with the complex interaction of nature and nurture, of the different ways in which people learn how to live in the world. Religion is as much about 'knowing how' as 'knowing that'—this acquisition of practical skills seems somehow missing or at least underplayed in the approach favoured by cognitive science. If we view religion as a striving after a practical wisdom, rather than acquiring a set of implausible beliefs about the supernatural, then the tasks of understanding and evaluation will need a more hands-on set of skills than those exhibited by evolutionary psychology.[30] Included will be the patient descriptions of ethnography, moral and aesthetic evaluation, historical perspective, and spiritual discernment. These more empathetic skills seem often absent in the writings of recent critics of religion. 'Understanding in practice is a process of *enskillment*, in which learning is inseparable from doing, and in which both are embedded in the context of a practical engagement in the world—that is, indwelling.'[31]

The term 'explanation', however, is also one that requires to be handled with caution. Explanation takes place relative to an interest. The 'why' question always has a context. Hilary Putnam gives the example of the famous thief Willie Sutton who was asked why he broke into banks. He replied 'Because that's where the money is'. The answer was true, of course, but it was not the explanation required.[32] In the case of evolutionary origins, to explain how something emerges in the past is not in itself to pronounce upon either its truth or its usefulness. This is the case not only in religion, but also with respect to science, art, music, and morality. These must have originated in ways that are deeply connected with our ancestral history and biological evolution. Why did Homo sapiens bury the dead (from about 200,000 years ago perhaps) and paint on the cave walls at Lascaux (about 13,000 years ago), alone of all the species? Answers to these questions will surely have important Darwinian elements. Yet an account of the origin of an idea or practice does not in itself tell us whether that idea is true or that practice good, let alone explain why they are so. In the case of mathematics, for example, it might be possible to give an account of how the brain has attained a facility for computational patterns, algorithmic functions, and abstract theorizing; these enable human beings to use mathematical concepts such as numbers from a very early age. However, this is the only the beginning of an adequate account. What a number really is, the nature of mathematical truths, and the reasons for their usefulness all require further explication. An understanding of these will require more than the methodologies of the natural sciences.

All scientific activity has its own institutional context and frame of reference. It takes place in relation to questions that are framed in particular ways and that are judged to be of importance within particular communities of enquiry. One does not need to accept some of the more extravagant claims of post-modernist writing to recognize the significance of context and perspective in all forms of academic study. Answers are offered in response to specific questions that are posed, and it is highly unlikely that these will remove the need for other forms of description and understanding when different questions are raised from other perspectives. The Olympian position adopted by recent work in evolutionary psychology of religion, often reinforced by publisher's blurb, is in danger of ignoring this broader context and hence of advocating an implausible narrowing of forms of human understanding.

The type of explanation offered by evolutionary accounts of religion tends generally to work downwards in a reductive direction by reducing the force of religion to its primeval sources. Religion imposes upon us, almost unwittingly, the belief that this world is ruled by supernatural agencies which can be accessed and in part controlled by the rituals, beliefs, and institutions of religions. It is akin to a virus that spreads amongst the population so that we have a situation in which people do not so much believe as believe in belief. We may not feel personally committed, but we are relieved that others do and are content that belief persists and flourishes in our societies. (This may explain the fear of criticism that breaks the spell.) The emergence of religion is generally perceived as a natural misfiring of otherwise healthy evolutionary drives and adaptive strategies. Note the discussion of HADD (hyper-active detection device), superstition, the bogus claims of shamans, and the ways in which organized religion spreads akin to a virus (memes). In much of the literature, cognitive science provides an error-theory for religion. It explains not only the ancestral origins of some religious habits, but also why exponents of religion today are generally mistaken about what is going on in their beliefs and rituals. Yet much of this is to beg the question against more emergentist patterns of explanation that see development and organization in human societies as requiring a more multi-dimensional set of descriptors. The following comments of anthropologist James Laidlaw may illustrate this.

Humanist study, as pursued alike by history and anthropology, cannot ignore the fact that in religion people have aimed at certain values and virtues, including and especially truth. To study the way they have variously invented, discovered, criticised, amended, defended, and have tried, succeeded, and failed to live up to and according to them, is necessarily at least in part to ask whether and to what extent, in doing so, they have realised their values and ideas. To seek instead to explain their beliefs and behaviour causally as the outcome of the mechanics of information processing errors, is just not to look them in the eye.[33]

As he suggests, an alternative way of looking at the phenomenon is available to someone who seeks to assess the power and force of religious faith as this is known to its practitioners. Biological explanations of the origins of our behaviour do not exclude this. We might equally well think in terms of new forms of explanation or description appearing with the increased complexity of cosmic evolution. These descriptive levels are not reducible to lower ones. No one type of explanation or source of knowledge should be privileged over all others. In the case of religion, art, and morality there may be forms of description that are required to provide an adequate account of what human beings understand themselves to be doing in these practices. This was part of Thomas Reid's response to David Hume in the eighteenth century. The world as we know it and life as we must live it require us to offer principles of explanation that do not reduce to a single method of enquiry or one type of knowledge.

Cognitive science has an important contribution to make towards our understanding of religion. Scholars of theology and religious studies will have to engage with it in the time ahead. But it is not the Holy Grail that will explain it away and remove the need for other forms of description, understanding, and explanation. These remain available and to this extent it is open to a theist to offer her own understanding of what happens at this stage of evolutionary complexity. The idea of God is not a by-product of the evolution of matter, essentially an illusory idea, a consequence of Darwinian misfiring. At any rate, this has not been shown. Other models become possible that appeal to emergent properties and patterns of explanation. Nor is the possibility of divine revelation excluded. Such claims will also require similar patterns of skilled appreciation, critical conversation, and practical discernment, often a troubling thought for anyone for whom the truth is simple, immediately accessible, and settled.

Notes

1. *Disturbing the Universe* (New York: Harper & Row, 1979), 250.
2. Cited by William E. Phipps, *Darwin's Religious Odyssey* (Harrisburg, PA: Trinity Press International, 2002), 51.
3. See John Bowlby, *Charles Darwin* (London: Pimlico, 1990), 228.
4. This is helpfully explored by Ernest McMullin, 'Cosmic Purpose and the Contingency of Human Evolution', *Theology Today*, 55 (1998/99), 389–414.

5. Simon Conway Morris, *Life's Solution: Inevitable Humans in a Lonely Universe* (Cambridge: Cambridge University Press, 2003), 232–3. For discussion see Holmes Ralston III, 'Inevitable Humans: Simon Conway Morris's Evolutionary Paleontology', *Zygon*, 40 (2005), 221–9.

6. See Philip E. Johnson, *Darwin on Trial* (Washington, DC: Regnery Gateway, 1991) and Michael Behe, *Darwin's Black Box* (New York: Free Press, 1996). For an accessible scientific rebuttal of creationism and ID theory see Kenneth Miller, *Finding Darwin's God: A Scientist's Search for Common Ground between God and Evolution* (Harper: New York, 1999).

7. See Barbara Forrest and Paul Gross, *Creationism's Trojan Horse: The Wedge of Intelligent Design* (Oxford: Oxford University Press, 2004).

8. Francis Collins, *The Language of God: A Scientist Presents Evidence for Belief* (New York: Free Press, 2006), 192. In what follows I am indebted to Collins.

9. Howard van Til, 'The Creation: Intelligently Designed or Optimally Equipped?', *Theology Today*, 55 (1998/9), 344–64 at 349.

10. Daniel Dennett, *Darwin's Dangerous Idea* (New York: Touchstone, 1995), 136.

11. *The Language of God*, 195.

12. For an overview of the field see Luther Martin, 'Religion and Cognition', in John Hinnells (ed.), *Routledge Companion to the Study of Religion* (London: Routledge, 2005), 473–88.

13. David M. Buss, 'Introduction', in Buss (ed.), *Handbook of Evolutionary Psychology* (Hoboken, NJ: Wiley & Sons, 2005), xxiv.

14. Pascal Boyer, *Religion Explained: The Human Instincts that Fashion Gods, Spirits and Ancestors* (London: Vintage, 2002).

15. Ibid., 74.

16. In the case of his own dog, Darwin notes this frequently fallacious but still useful intentional agency. See *The Descent of Man* (London: Penguin, 2004), 118.

17. Scott Atran, *In Gods We Trust: The Evolutionary Landscape of Religion* (New York: Oxford University Press, 2002), 266.

18. Boyer, *Religion Explained*, 178.

19. Dennett, *Darwin's Dangerous Idea*, 180.

20. Dennett, *Breaking the Spell: Religion as a Natural Phenomenon* (London: Penguin, 2007), 108.

21. See Boyer, *Religion Explained*, 189ff.

22. Scott Atran, *In Gods We Trust*, 274ff. Atran suggests the possibility of a continued co-existence of science and religion, although this seems largely on the basis of naturalist claims about the role of religion. The explanation tends in a downwards direction with little scope for complementarity.

23. 'Once people entertain a particular hypothesis, they tend to detect and recall positive instances that seem to confirm it, but they are often less good at detecting possible refutation.' Boyer, *Religion Explained*, 346.

24. This is the direction taken by Justin L. Barrett, *Why Would Anyone Believe in God?* (Lanham, MD: Altamira Press, 2004).

25. 'Your view as to what sort of creature a human being is will determine or at any rate heavily influence your views as to what it is rational or irrational for human beings to believe. But the answer to that question depends on whether or not Christian theism is true. And so the dispute as to whether theistic belief is rational, in the present sense, cannot be settled just by attending to epistemological considerations; it is at bottom not merely an epistemological dispute, but a metaphysical or theological dispute.' Alvin Plantinga, 'Religion and Epistemology', in Edward Craig (ed.), *Routledge Encyclopedia of Philosophy* (London: Routledge, 1998), Vol. 8, 209–17.

26. *Religion Explained*, 369.

27. Simon Conway Morris, *Life's Solution*, 324.

28. For a useful criticism of memetic theory in this context see Alister McGrath, *Dawkins' God: Genes, Memes and the Meaning of Life* (Oxford: Blackwell, 2005), 119ff.

29. Tim Ingold, 'From the Transmission of Representations to the Education of Attention', in Harvey Whitehouse (ed.), *The Debated Mind: Evolutionary Psychology versus Ethnography* (Oxford: Berg, 2001), 113–54 at 132.

30. For a recent account of the significance of wisdom in theology see David Ford, *Christian Wisdom: Desiring God and Learning in Love* (Cambridge: Cambridge University Press, 2007). In exploring the comprehensive nature of wisdom, Ford illustrates the need for a cross-disciplinary series of conversations in the study of religion.

31. Tim Ingold, 'Epilogue', in Kathleen R. Gibson and Tim Ingold (eds.), *Tools, Language and Cognition in Human Evolution* (Cambridge: Cambridge University Press, 1993), 447–72 at 463.

32. Hilary Putnam, *Meaning and the Moral Sciences* (London: Routledge & Kegan Paul, 1978), 42.
33. James Laidlaw, 'A Well-Disposed Anthropologist's Problems with the "Cognitive Science of Religion"', in Harvey Whitehouse and James Laidlaw (eds.), *Religion, Anthropology and Cognitive Science* (Durham, NC: Carolina Academic Press, 2007), 211–46 at 231.

4

MORALITY, ART, AND RELIGION: INVENTION OR DISCOVERY?

A dominant feature of my argument against recent criticism of religion is that patterns of explanation and description should not be flattened or levelled out in favour of one single type. No solitary approach or discipline can provide a complete account. Despite this, many neo-Darwinian accounts tend to favour a comprehensive materialist explanation of social phenomena, including religion. This ideological expansion of Darwinian explanation is presumably why evolutionary theory is viewed (wrongly) with such suspicion by large sectors of the public. Against this, we should allow a multi-layered series of descriptions that provide a richer and more adequate account of what we typically do and believe. This does not of course amount to proof of religion or theism, but it does create the space within which it can be evaluated fairly in its own terms and in light of what its practitioners say and do.

Against neo-Darwinian materialism, religion typically moves further downwards and upwards in its descriptive patterns. Where materialism argues that the physical universe is a sheer brute fact, religion will seek to offer an account of cosmic origins that is characterized by intention, purpose, and reason. In this respect, the explanation resists matter as its terminal point. At the same time, explanation also has an upwards movement. As a result of evolving life forms new patterns of description become possible. These include the language of consciousness, morality, art, and religion, not to mention the activity of science itself. As the cosmos evolves, so new patterns of description emerge. It was for this reason that many late-nineteenth-century scholars saw Darwinism not as narrowly materialist but as representing a rich, fruitful, and beautiful vision. The attempt to characterize social life in purely neo-Darwinian terms needs therefore to be contested in favour of emergent and non-reducible types of description that employ personal, moral, aesthetic, and religious categories. It is significant that these are also the sorts of category employed to characterize the lowest form of description for cosmic origins, i.e. creation by God. There is thus a categorial correlation of explanatory models in terms of first cause and final end.

This rather abstract thought might be illustrated by reference to liturgical, credal, and catechetical language. The Eucharistic prayer of the Scottish Episcopal Church speaks of God as 'source and final purpose'. The ancient creeds begin with a confession of God as creator and conclude with an affirmation of eternal life. The Shorter Catechism, which generations of Scots had to memorize, opens with the statement that our 'chief end is to glorify God and enjoy him forever'. The danger in this language is that it tends to prioritize a type of intellectual contemplation over practice. Knowing is privileged above doing. For philosophers and theologians who spend a lot of time thinking, this is a besetting temptation. By contrast, the language of prayer in all the Abrahamic faiths exhibits a pattern of confession followed by practical imperative. This is especially evident in the Hebrew Psalms. Since God our Maker is like this and has done that, so we must live in this way and according to these precepts.

Consider the following scenario that draws upon what the pragmatist philosopher C. S. Peirce called a 'neglected argument' for the existence of God.[1] It is inevitable that human beings with their capacity for self-consciousness, reflection, and search for ultimate meanings will entertain the concept of God, namely the notion of a supreme being. This God, *ex hypothesi*, is the source and end of all things, the origin of all that we value and cherish, the knowledge and worship of whom is our highest end. Even beginning on a constructivist basis, Peirce notes that we incline towards this idea through investigating, contemplating, and perhaps yearning for its truthfulness. Moreover, we will gradually be struck by its capacity to organize the different aspects of our intellectual life, to provide a unifying goal of practical life, and generally to ameliorate the human condition. The usefulness of the concept of God is not easily dispelled simply by giving a plausible account of how hominid evolution predisposed us towards developing the notion. We might even view this as providential. Once established, we are compelled to explore this notion and to assess its worth. In this way, religion can get going as an activity or form of life that resists the downwards pressure of an inflated evolutionary psychology. It requires assessment not only in terms of its historical origins but also its truthfulness. The question of the latter will remain even if we can produce a satisfactory account of the former. The same goes for science itself, including evolutionary psychology. We can provide an explanatory account of how human beings have developed the capacity for scientific understanding and technological achievement, yet this does not absolve us from the assessment of competing scientific theories. An account of genetic origins must be consistent with rational discrimination, otherwise evolutionary psychology itself would become a self-defeating enterprise.[2]

As religion or more specifically the idea of God impresses as true, useful, and compelling, then other forms of explanation become available and internal to the self-understanding of the religious practitioner. In particular, the argument that this is the way in which the sense of God emerges within the evolution of the human race now requires inspection. While there are formidable difficulties confronting such a move, it cannot simply be excluded as redundant by virtue of the power of scientific explanation. In what follows, a complementary and non-competitive type of account is offered that seeks to provide 'added value'. In appealing to a further dimension of understanding, the argument seeks to integrate and offer a unified explanation of what happens at other levels including that of biological evolution.

Sociobiology and Ethics

Anyone arguing for emergent levels of explanation would be well advised to seek examples of these other than the religious. Having some companions in guilt will strengthen the thesis, and there are in any case some interesting parallels in the case of art and morality with respect to their evolutionary origins. These too, it will be argued, resist a downwards Darwinian explanation. In doing so, they contribute to a richer and more multi-faceted account of the world and human life.

Much of the discussion generated by the new atheism revolves around the issue of whether you need to be religious to be moral. Often quoted in this context is Dostoevsky's dictum that 'if God does not exist, then everything is permitted'. Here the thought seems to be that morals will lose their foundation and sanction, where they cease to repose upon some transcendent reality. So the loss of religious belief and the social cohesion that accompanies it results in a diminished ethical commitment. Without the sanctions of religion, our moral fibre is weakened. Stated in this way, the argument is suspect for several reasons. Dawkins and others have little difficulty in disposing of it. For example, there is a striking degree of

commonality between the moral commitments of those across
and outside faith communities. Pluralist societies could not
function without significant degrees of cooperation and consensus between their members, whether of different faiths or
none. Too much attention to moral quandaries over abortion,
euthanasia, capital punishment, and so on can obscure the
extensive range of shared commitments. In this context, Jeffrey
Stout has pointed to the moral platitudes of the nursery where
small children are taught to be considerate, cooperative, and
polite and to desist from forms of behaviour that are vindictive,
selfish, or violent.[3] These platitudes are inculcated whether the
nursery is Catholic, Jewish, or secular. Moreover, arguments
that move from moral objectivity to God are usually much
too swift. Non-theistic outlooks such as Confucianism and
Buddhism are deeply ethical and have sustained moral traditions over many centuries. This has been achieved religiously
but not theistically. The claim that only God can guarantee
morality has a somewhat parochial and western register in this
respect. And, in any case, it is not difficult to identify significant moral exemplars such as Nelson Mandela whose commitments have not been religiously grounded. David Hume
too, it seems, was a fine human being. Indeed, in some cases,
the loss of faith may result in an intensified devotion to social
and political ends. The sons and daughters of manses have
often distinguished themselves morally and intellectually while
adhering only loosely or not at all to the faith of their upbringing. The blogging generated by Dawkins and others reveals
quite understandably the hostility that is aroused by those who
seek to impugn the moral credentials of secularists. Hence, it
would be as well for religious apologists to drop this argument
in the form in which it frequently appears.

Nevertheless, the relation of scientific explanation to other
types is raised by our moral beliefs and commitments. The
discipline of sociobiology claims to offer an account of the
evolutionary origins of morality in terms of the advantage

that altruistic behaviour confers upon the survival of our genes.[4] Dawkins himself has made an important contribution to this field of study in his most celebrated book *The Selfish Gene*.[5] This metaphor is often thought to imply the inherent selfishness of organisms but this is a mistake. Genetic drives promote forms of cooperation amongst individuals thus resulting in non-selfish and even sacrificial patterns of behaviour. Hence the selfish gene can produce an altruistic phenotype and community. How does this work? Given the urge towards reproducing one's own genes, will individuals not seek advantage over others where that can be secured? This creates a prima facie instability in evolutionary adaptability. To flourish the group requires patterns of cooperation, yet it seems that the individual will always be genetically driven to seek an advantage over against others where the opportunity arises. How is this resolved? Sociobiology emerged in the 1960s following important work on insect groups. William Hamilton's work on hymenoptera (ants, bees, and wasps) shows how workers can further their own biological interests by serving the group. Their genetic survival is best ensured not so much by individual acts of reproduction as by securing the position of other members of the group to whom they are closely related, particularly their genetic sisters. Known as kin selection, this principle provides a useful way of resolving the apparent tension between individual and group interests.[6]

Other models for explaining biological altruism include reciprocal altruism which, drawing on concepts from game theory, can show how reproduction is best facilitated in given circumstances by strategies in which each conforms to cooperative norms. This back-scratching rationale is a vital component of genetic survival. This has led to more recent attention to group altruism in which other-regarding behaviour has the objective of promoting the survival and reproduction not just of one's offspring or kin but of one's own group. Groups of altruists, it is alleged, are over the long run likely to do better than associations of more 'selfish' types. Thus a tendency to seek out the company of other altruists and to support them may have a biological explanation in some animal populations. Group cooperation facilitates survival; therefore, membership of a cooperative is more likely to secure one's genetic line. This is not reducible to reciprocal altruism but requires more sophisticated accounts of group selection and adaptive strategies that evolve within successful groups.

In applying this type of explanation to human societies, sociobiology has encountered some opposition. There are various anxieties that typically occasion resistance. Earlier philosophies of Darwinism and their links to eugenics have aroused suspicion whenever biological forms of explanation have been extended to human societies. Recent historical work reveals how widespread and insidious were eugenic strategies not only amongst Nazis.[7] However, it would be unfair to taint recent sociobiology as an extension of Darwinian science simply on account of grotesque ideological corruptions from early periods. The attempt to offer sociobiological explanation is grounded in experimental work and has some explanatory and predictive power. It should have a legitimate place in our understanding of how we function as social beings, without seeking normative or ideological status. Recent research has shown how family relationships and social customs may be determined by strategies of reciprocal altruism. Perhaps the best-known example of its success has been to expose the strikingly different homicide rates between the children of stepfathers and those of natural fathers. This phenomenon is apparent in the animal world where, for example, male lions will kill the young of another female when she is co-opted as a mate. Research now suggests that it has an analogue in human societies. Only after the research of Daly and Wilson in 1988 brought this to light did police forces distinguish cases of murder between biological and social parents.[8]

However, significant problems confront a complete socio-biological explanation of moral behaviour. The rhetoric of selfishness may itself be over-worked and somewhat misleading. It is genes rather than individual organisms that are described as selfish. So actions are not consciously intended towards selfish ends, in our normal use of that concept. In any case, it has been pointed out that the drive towards genetic production is in other respects not at all narrowly 'selfish'. In sexual reproduction, we are typically looking at divisions and new combinations of genes in which each partner contributes only one half. The drive towards reproduction, moreover, assists the species and the evolutionary process when considered on a more holistic scale. In this process, individual organisms will often put themselves at a disadvantage for the sake of their offspring. All of this can be accommodated by the sociobiologist, yet it may suggest that the language of 'selfishness' needs to be complemented by other metaphorical descriptions of what happens as a result of our biological drives. In a foreword to a new edition of *The Selfish Gene*, Dawkins himself suggests that the metaphor of 'the *cooperative* gene' might work just as well.

Studies of kin altruism can account in some measure for the disposition and affections we display towards those to whom we are closely related. It has also been suggested that it might explain a general propensity towards forms of nepotism, whether in ancient tribal systems or the House of Commons. And it may also reveal why proponents of such behaviour seem to regard a preference for their relatives as quite natural. Yet even in the case of kin altruism, actions that are for the benefit of one's genetic survival are also always for the benefit of someone else's genetic survival. And sometimes the shared genetic material is very much less than 50 per cent. So the rhetoric of selfishness requires some qualification.

In the case of group altruism, the descriptions offered are more wide-ranging and comprehensive. There is less burden on showing that cooperative activity is with those to whom we are genetically related. Wider patterns of altruism can be detected in insect, fish, bird, and mammal populations that seem to require a broader scope of explanation. Group selection can provide this. For example, research amongst chimpanzees has shown how patterns of grooming and food-sharing are conditioned by recollection of past favours and the expectation of future reciprocation. This 'altruistic' behaviour will tend to place the well-regulated group at an adaptive advantage over others. In the case of flocks of birds, it can be shown statistically that those flocks with more individuals who selflessly draw attention to predators will tend to fare better than other flocks with a preponderance of selfish non-callers.[9] When applied to human societies, however, the theory of group selection requires greater complexity to accommodate altruism across groups and the manner in which ideas are culturally transmitted. Here appeal is made to meme theory—'memes' being those ideas or cultural artefacts that are transmitted across populations in ways that best ensure their survival and replication.

A leading exponent of group selection theory, David Wilson, has sought to extend the scope of the theory to human behaviour and the capacity of religious ideas and precepts to ensure the survival and prosperity of a group. In his book *Darwin's Cathedral*, he offers a striking study of Geneva under John Calvin as confirming the theory. The theology and moral practices that were rigorously developed in Protestant Switzerland make good sense in terms of a theory of group selection. Genevan society with its system of enforced belief, church discipline, and out-group hostility provides a powerful example of the capacity of religion to advance group selection. This religion, therefore, exhibits an impressive adaptive complexity under specific historic conditions.

The precepts of the Genevan catechism draw upon moral norms that are held to be universally valid, but apply these to

the social condition of the city. This ensures both the regulation of the conduct of the general population and also a system
in which the authorities themselves are constrained to serve
the needs of the group, rather than their own private ends.
The beliefs that are articulated in Calvin's theology provide
heavy reinforcement of this code of conduct, particularly his
account of an embattled company of the elect resisting the
forces of Antichrist and persevering until death when it enters
into its eternal reward. The rigorous system of church and civil
discipline, moreover, ensures that free-riders and cheats who
threaten the cohesion of the group are harshly treated and thus
discouraged. At the same time, any exterior force threatening
the group, for example the teaching of Michael Servetus, is res-
olutely exposed and punished, if necessary by execution. Sum-
marizing his account, Wilson writes, 'Calvin's church included
a code of behaviors adapted to the local environment, a belief
system that powerfully motivated the code inside the mind of
the believer, and a social organization that coordinated and
enforced the code for leaders and followers alike.'[10]

What does one do with this account? In many ways, it
is impressive although it merely confirms what historians
have often said about the ways in which Protestant communities in Strasbourg, Geneva, and elsewhere required to
be cohesive and tightly disciplined in order to survive. In
other respects, however, it simply discards the careful scrutiny
of belief, the detailed debates surrounding predestination in
which Calvin engaged with his opponents, and the subsequent ways in which the Protestant tradition felt intellectually and morally compelled to adjust Calvin's theology on
this matter. For Wilson's account, these must be epiphenom-
ena when compared to the strong evolutionary forces that
shape the beliefs and practices of the group for the sake of
their survival. The capacity of a community to engage in a
process of internal reasoning and external debate about the

plausibility and validity of its truth claims is here largely ignored.

This takes us to a deeper form of anxiety that surrounds the extent to which the discipline of sociobiology tends towards a reductive explanation of morality. Roughly speaking, the unease is around the notion that our cooperative instincts are simply the result of evolutionary conditioning and that there is nothing valuable about altruism beyond its capacity to ensure the survival of our genes. The ethical evaluations we make seem like illusions that nature has tricked us into believing. Yet our intuition is to hold that morality has a purpose and a claim upon us that are not exhausted by the evolutionary advantages that it confers. To reduce it in this way might be regarded as a clear instance of the so-called 'naturalistic fallacy', which reduces ethical properties to natural ones thus eliminating key moral concepts such as 'goodness', 'duty', and the 'ought' of moral imperatives.

Before pressing this button, however, we need to consider the ways in which sociobiology can render quite a good account of much of our social life. We cooperate with others because it is basically good for us and for them. Here again the great thinkers of the Scottish Enlightenment have something to offer. In observing patterns of economic transaction, Adam Smith noted how the extensive forms of cooperation in daily commerce took place largely in accordance with the pursuit of one's own interests. These were not to be interpreted narrowly since almost everyone had friends, family, and neighbours to whom they were naturally attached. Nevertheless, as he said famously in *The Wealth of Nations*, 'Give me that which I want and you shall have this which you want...it is in this manner that we obtain from one another the far greater good of those good offices which we stand in need of. It is not from the benevolence of the butcher, the brewer, or the baker, that we expect our dinner, but from their regard to their own interest.'[11] The only mistake that Smith appears to have made here is to assume that animals are incapable of similar patterns of successful cooperation. He records the report of travellers that baboons cooperated in robbing orchards in the Cape of Good Hope but then fought to death over the spoils.[12]

Theologians too have been conscious that the conditions of human life are such that our most selfish and corrupt instincts tend to be curbed by the natural order that promotes a measure of peace and cooperation. In Augustine's *City of God*, a bleak account is offered of our condition after the fall of Adam and Eve. Yet even in the earthly city which is marked by disordered desire and competing interests there exist constraints that enable commerce, political rule, and the growth of civilization. In speaking variously of natural law and common grace, Catholic and Protestant theology alike have recognized that even outside the church cooperation and civil conduct are both necessary and achievable for the flourishing of societies.

David Hume offered an account of justice in terms of its capacity to ameliorate a situation of limited goods and restricted sympathies. To enable the regulation of society we need a system of justice to which each commits. The temptation to be a free-rider must be diminished by the imposition of a series of sanctions. In this respect, a social morality is something that we devise in order to improve the human situation. We imagine that there must be more to it, but this is an illusion that is naturally engendered by our tendency to stain the world with the colours of the mind.[13] It is no coincidence that evolutionary ethics today employs very similar language. 'Ethics is a collective illusion of the genes put in place to make good co-operators. Nothing more, but also nothing less.'[14] This theory of morality sits quite well with sociobiological accounts of its evolutionary origins. It makes sense of the point of morality from the perspective of each agent and why it is in our own interests to promote the social virtues. In addition, Hume's reading of our intuitions about moral objectivity might be explained naturalistically on the basis that these are useful mental fictions that advantage our social condition. So it is not surprising to find a modern philosopher like J. L. Mackie associating his Humean account of morality with an explanation of why we tend to over-determine the notion of moral objectivity. 'If we admit what Hume calls the mind's "propensity to spread itself on external objects", we can understand the supposed objectivity of moral qualities as arising from what we can call the projection or objectification of moral attributes.'[15]

But does this work as an account of our moral intuitions, reasoning, and commitments? At the very least, it creates some disturbance in the way we regard the 'objectivity' of ethical judgements. In fairness to Mackie and others, it should be noted that they are often quite up-front about this. The idea that the world out there is characterized by moral properties is one that is delusory and in any case difficult to explicate. Realism has thus to be abandoned in favour of some form of anti- or quasi-realism, a set of theories that offer an account of moral standards as devised for social amelioration. With their long ancestral reinforcement, we imagine, often quite usefully, that our moral standards are somehow written into the fabric of the universe. But the combination of scepticism and naturalism renders this impossible.

Nevertheless, the problems attaching to this view, especially when harnessed to sociobiological explanation, are quite formidable. Our moral discourse typically suggests that we are reasoning about something that can be discovered, as opposed merely to seeking out strategies to maximize group survival. We think, argue, and act with the conviction that moral judgements have a truth value that is not of our own making. The process of argumentation, sometimes leading to moral conversion, confirms our impression that there are moral facts that have nothing to do with the future of one's genes.

A particular difficulty facing evolutionary ethics is to explain the universal demands of justice and compassion. What was the Good Samaritan doing in assisting a member of an out-group, someone whose clan was at enmity with his own? Was he deluded by his moral principles in offering mercy to a stricken Jew, a case of evolutionary misfiring, a curious spandrel of human behaviour requiring explanation by a cognitive psychologist? Perhaps there is some concealed and indirect advantage to himself and his kin in his action. Much has been written on this, but his principle of charity—recognized by most moral traditions as generous and right—is not easily explained on evolutionary grounds. At this level of interpersonal encounter, another set of concepts and considerations comes into play over and above a story about biological interests and genetic drives. At times, the claims of other persons upon us may conflict directly with our own narrow advantage. Much of the teaching of Jesus seems to collide with the demands of natural selection and to most of us it seems none the worse for it. The divine commonwealth comprises not our genetic relatives but those who are committed to do the will of God. Eunuchs are praised for placing the demands of faith above those of their biological nature. We are commanded to love our enemies, strangers, and foreigners—all the out-groups who are distanced from our kith, kin, and co-religionists.

One might try to close the gap between our natural interests and the moral demands placed upon us. Yet, however blurred this dividing line, there seems to be a fundamental difference between being moved to act in one's own natural interests and being moved to act in accordance with principles of justice and mercy. A tradition of thought running through Duns Scotus, Reid, and Kant distinguishes two fundamentally different principles of action, an affection for justice and an affection for advantage.[16] Self-love, as the pursuit of happiness, is in itself a right and worthy motive. It may include the happiness of those most closely affiliated to us. Yet there is another principle by which it must be regulated and to which it is subordinate, which is the affection for justice. Kant labelled it the categorical imperative, while locating God in a rather different way. This gap between the natural and the moral is crucial to the way we regard the world and ourselves. The attempt by evolutionary ethics to close it compromises much that is vital to our humanity. It is not coincidental that when Thomas Reid responded to Hume's ethical naturalism he made a similar distinction between two fundamentally different principles of action—self-love and justice. From childhood, we recognize these to be motivated quite separately and it is simply a confusion to attempt to reduce the latter to the former as Hume does in his account of justice as an artificial virtue.

It is of course open to the Darwinian ethicist to offer a deflated account of our moral intuitions that still leaves sufficient intact for people to behave in a civilized fashion. Different strategies have been attempted, yet much of the way we think and behave is exposed as confused and illusory by the downwards direction of the explanation. 'Morality', it is said, 'is a collective illusion foisted upon us by our genes.'[17] Yet a richer explanation is available by moving in an upwards direction to acknowledge that as self-conscious, reflective agents we are capable of apprehending and to some degree acting upon moral truth claims. Here one can argue that self-consciousness is always accompanied by an awareness of other persons as similarly constituted and making claims upon us. The Other is the one to whom we are bound personally and not merely biologically, socially, or economically. Hegel's analysis of the instability of the master–slave relationship illustrates the importance of reciprocity and equality in human affairs. As self-consciousness arises in human beings, we require recognition and acceptance to be freely offered by others. Without a moral structuring of our relationships, this cannot be achieved. At this level of human evolution, another vocabulary is necessary to account for the ethical life in which we are ineluctably involved. This presupposes the biological but cannot be reduced to it.

One curious feature of this debate is that it tends to assume that altruism is difficult to explain. Egoism is the unproblematic default position that seems intuitively right. If we can relate altruism in some way to our egoistic desires then we can account for it. Yet perhaps this is a parochial assumption. When confronted with this debate, students from non-western cultures typically express some bafflement. African and Asian traditions see people not as atomized individuals but as existing only in and through a network of connections with other people. Mandela and Tutu have made much of the African concept of 'ubuntu', which recognizes the social and personal bonds that make us who we are as people. Even in western philosophy, there have been attempts to develop more personalist notions of the self. John Macmurray writes of how the human person can only be thought of in relation to other persons. There is no 'I' without a 'You', no self except in relation to the other. The concept of the person requires categories of intentionality, freedom, friendship, and love. These cannot be reduced to biological or organic terms.[18]

This observation might require us to qualify Adam Smith's observation, noted earlier, about our reliance upon the self-interest of the butcher, baker, and brewer. We must presuppose this, but is there not also a degree of trust present in them as persons which in turn requires some tokens of respect and recognition? Our commercial relationships are never entirely disjoined from the personal dimension, and this intensifies where the relationship is not so much one of supplier to consumer but teacher to pupil, doctor to patient, counsellor to client. The local chip shop may have the best fish supper in town but if I am not shown courtesy from behind the counter then I am unlikely to be a regular customer. Similarly, without respect on my part, my business is unlikely to be valued. Market principles cannot be abstractly divorced from the wider personal dimension and the ethical claims that are made upon us.

Smith himself made a notable contribution to discussion of moral sentiments, arguing that the principle of sympathy was part of our human constitution. Here one might see greater continuity between the evolutionary origins of morality and our intuitive commitment to moral objectivity. A good evolutionary account of our cooperative and sympathetic tendencies might be offered, but this is the beginning not the end of moral perception. Evolution is enabling. It facilitates patterns of moral discernment, reasoning, and criticism that do not reduce to survival mechanisms. Yet without these mechanisms we would not have acquired the capacities of moral agents. Much recent research on non-human primates seems to confirm that our moral propensities have been endowed in part by nature. Chimpanzees for example often display an empathy with their companions. This emotional contagion enables the animals to understand the feelings of others. Closely related is the mechanism of sympathy that comprises feelings of compassion for a needy or distressed other.[19] This generates socially cooperative behaviour that is not always based on calculations about reciprocity. This extends to targeted helping and to offering consolation in times of crisis or trouble. Frans de Waal's intriguing study of empathy amongst the primates includes a wide range of evidence for this, documenting the extent to which shared affections can induce sympathetic behaviour. One of his most striking photographs is of a young chimpanzee attempting to put its consoling arm around a screaming elder male who has just been defeated in a fight.[20]

The case of Richard Dawkins is interesting here. While dismissing the significance of religion for ethics, he is also adamant that the forces of natural selection cannot provide an adequate basis for human morality. Here he bristles with that same defiant moral passion that marked Bertrand Russell's atheism. Yet, this moral concern actually subverts or at least transcends Darwinian explanation. What it suggests is that while evolutionary forces may have generated powers of empathy and moral reasoning in human societies, these then have a capacity for more independent reflection and assessment that is not bound by evolutionary drives. This point is made by Peter Singer in his discussion of de Waal's work on animal behaviour.

Though a capacity to reason helps us to survive and reproduce, once we develop a capacity for reasoning, we may be led by it to places that are not of any direct advantage to us, in evolutionary terms. Reason is like an escalator—once we step on it, we cannot get off until we have gone where it takes us. An ability to count can be useful, but it leads by a logical process to the abstractions of higher mathematics that have no direct payoff in evolutionary terms.[21]

Aesthetic Realism

What about art? In some ways, this may illustrate much more clearly than either religion or ethics both the validity and limits of Darwinian explanation. A genetic evolutionary account of our capacity for aesthetic judgements has much to offer but is unlikely to prove exhaustive in accounting for our standards and practice.

Sex selection, as Darwin claimed, may explain in evolutionary terms the beauty of the peacock's tail. Its colours are a sign of health and strength to a potential mate. In finding them attractive, the peahen selects the brightest available breeding partner. The principle of natural selection can thus explain why the peacock has such an ornate tail. In some respects, it may not render the peacock particularly well adapted to survival since it will be more readily detectable by predators. Yet, it does apparently promote the reproduction of its genes. The other main component of the explanation is of course the attraction felt by the peacock's mate. Her allurement is determined by an instinctive sense that the bright colours are emblematic of strength and fitness for breeding. For many evolutionary psychologists, this sexual attraction to what is bright, colourful, and patterned is the origin of our aesthetic sense. Darwin himself speculates in *The Descent of Man* that some ingrained preference for regularity and symmetry must account for the pleasure excited by bright colours and the picturesque displays performed during mating.[22] But how far does this account for our own aesthetic preferences and judgements? A degree of attraction, sometimes erotic, is doubtless present in responses to visual art. Yet it seems that the genetic origins of such attraction do little to explain the standards of judgement we invoke.

In his acclaimed study of the human mind, Stephen Pinker offers a fuller sociobiological view. Aesthetic concerns are a function of the brain's circuitry that ultimately promote survival. The idea here is that the curiosity and search for connections that are so useful in enabling us to survive and prosper also facilitate aesthetic interests. He distinguishes between the *pleasure* derived from aesthetic objects and their *utility* in evolutionary terms. These are related of course by virtue of the stimuli derived from thoughts and sensations that have survival advantages. 'Music', he writes, is 'auditory cheesecake, an exquisite confection crafted to tickle the sensitive spots of at least six of our mental faculties.'[23] These comprise the following: language that is heightened when it becomes song; the auditory organization of the world around us; the emotional calls from other persons; habitat selection (sounds can signify safe or unsafe habitats—just consider the theme music from *Jaws*); control of our motor functions as expressed through rhythm and dance; and a further ingredient that he describes as the whole together offering more than the sum of its parts. As in similar studies of religion, these survival mechanisms combine to produce artistic phenomena. What is significant here is the way in which his evolutionary explanation works downwards towards eliminating higher forms of explanation of aesthetic phenomena. Other types of explanation may explain shifting and contrasting tastes but these allow the evolutionary model to remain in pole position.

David Sloan Wilson again writes briskly, 'We are emotionally attracted to features of the physical and social environment that are likely to increase our fitness, which we experience as beautiful.'[24] The standards that we invoke appeal to something like a consensus on artistic matters. This regulates our judgements and provides training in aesthetics. But to presuppose an aesthetic realism is again to stain and gild the world with the colours of the mind. There is nothing out there corresponding to aesthetic judgements. All that can be appealed to is some ideal, universal standard of human taste. A painting may thus be praised for its harmony, its use of colour, its technical accomplishments, and its capacity consistently to arouse our pleasure, fascination, and admiration. On this view, an artistic judgement is finally non-cognitive, expressing at bottom a human sensory reaction to an artefact.

However, this hedonistic account of artistic judgement seems not entirely to account for the necessary qualities of universality and disinterestedness that many critics would regard as essential in aesthetics. While there may be some evolutionary pushes in that direction, a richer account of aesthetic judgement needs to move in a more realist direction to invoke the language of discovery, disclosure, and understanding. A reductive theory might do service as an account of standards of taste in food and wine, but it functions less well in literature and music where a more developed grammar of aesthetic discernment has to be learned. To view music as little more than 'auditory cheesecake' seems to miss something important. The sense of constraint and discovery that characterize the work of the artist is better explained by an account of the world as in some sense possessing the qualities or dimensions that are displayed by a work of art. To that extent, what is represented is not so much invented as uncovered or brought to light.

Iris Murdoch writes of the quasi-religious nature of art in terms of such a realism of judgement.

Good art, thought of as a symbolic force rather than statement provides a stirring image of a pure, transcendent value, a steadily visible enduring higher good, and perhaps provides for many people, in an unreligious age without prayer or sacraments, their clearest experience of something grasped as separate and precious and beneficial and held quietly, and unpossessively in the attention.[25]

She goes on to argue that art is a discerning exercise in relation to the real. Essential to the judgements we make is the notion of revelation, the really real, 'the world as we were never able so clearly to see it before'.[26] Murdoch's vision of art of course is notoriously austere. It does not allow much for playfulness, celebration, and entertainment, qualities that can also be found in 'good' art as for example Mozart's *Marriage of Figaro* or Shakespeare's *Midsummer Night's Dream*. Nevertheless, the sense of being led beyond oneself and the more mundane aspects of life is evident at concerts, exhibitions, and book festivals. 'The calm joy in the picture gallery', she writes, 'is quite unlike the pleasurable flutter in the sale room.'[27]

This aesthetic realism is hard to describe beyond a few images and general ideas, although it belonged to Plato's three transcendentals of goodness, beauty, and truth. It is often abandoned in favour of something less metaphysically peculiar and extravagant, more Humean perhaps in orientation. Yet philosophers such as Thomas Reid felt compelled to locate artistic values in the being of God as this was mediated in created realities. This was not the result of an indulgent habit of metaphysical speculation, so much as arising from the conviction that our ordinary judgements and ways of speaking about aesthetic properties could not otherwise be understood. In this respect, Reidian realism was an attempt to return to premodern accounts that stressed the objective aesthetic qualities of the created world which the mind when properly ordered could apprehend. Beauty was the aesthetic mode of appearance of what was good and true. While eighteenth-century writers tended to stress the constructive responses of the mind to the data of perception, Reid sought to establish artistic judgement as a cognitive recognition of the way the world was constituted. Unlike Kant, artistic apprehension was closely related in Reid to the moral perception of our having duties that could not be reduced to disguised forms of self-interest.

Another celebrated example of this move towards an aesthetic realism is in Martin Heidegger's 1935 essay on 'The Origin of the Work of Art'. There he claims that art cannot be accounted for in terms of simply representing the world. Nor can it be described in terms of creating objects that arouse pleasure or desire, or incite us to action. Instead art can only be characterized by the notion of uncovering or disclosure. It is closely related to the Greek concept of truth (*aletheia*). A Greek temple does not represent anything, he argues, but instead opens up for us a world in which we find ourselves. It reveals the earth, the sky, and the sacred, and in doing so discloses to us something of our transient lives amidst these forces. He also considers in some detail Van Gogh's painting of a pair of peasant shoes. The painting reveals to us something that cannot be described in scientific terms. It is not so much that they are objects of beauty that arouse desire. They tell a story that locates them in a wider context and in which their significance comes to light.

From the dark opening of the worn insides of the shoes the toilsome tread of the worker stares forth. In the stiffly rugged heaviness of the shoes there is the accumulated tenacity of her slow trudge through

the far-spreading and ever-uniform furrows of the field swept by
a raw wind. On the leather lie the dampness and richness of the
soil. Under the soles stretches the loneliness of the field-path as
evening falls. In the shoes vibrates the silent call of the earth, its
quiet gift of the ripening grain and its unexplained self-refusal in
the fallow desolation of the wintry field. This equipment is per-
vaded by uncomplaining worry as to the certainty of bread, the
wordless joy of having once more withstood want, the trembling
before the impending childhood and shivering at the surrounding
menace of death... The artwork lets us know what shoes are in
truth.[28]

For the present context, Heidegger's discussion is significant in
two ways. First, art is about truth, unfolding, and discovery. It
cannot be reduced to a category of invention or construction.
It has a quality of showing forth or laying bare that is not
captured by accounts such as that of neo-Darwinism. And,
second, the truth that is here disclosed cannot be expressed
adequately in non-artistic form. The aesthetic medium and its
message are really inseparable. At most, the critic can offer an
account of what is being shown but this is never an account
that can substitute for the work itself, whether it is a painting,
a poem, or a musical performance.

What I am *not* seeking to argue is that there is a straight
and swift path from aesthetic realism to God. The theist will
doubtless have something to say about this connection, but the
argument here is that while Darwinism will offer an account of
the evolutionary origins of artistic practice, it ceases to explain
what is going on when one moves to culture, language, and
the kind of activity that is involved in aesthetics. There are
different versions of aesthetic realism on offer, some of them
more Platonic and non-theistic, and my claim is only that some
account of artistic disclosure is required to explain much that
is familiar to us in aesthetic judgement.

The thesis that aesthetic sentiments are judgements rather
than accounts of feelings or educated standards of taste makes
sense of the significant energy and resources that are invested

in literature, art, and music, and more importantly of the critical vocabulary for discrimination and the arguments that are frequently employed. At root here is the conviction that in artistic forms, or at least some of them, the world reveals itself to us.[29] An intuitive sense of our understanding being enhanced or transformed, as well as our deliberations over great art, counts against the dictum that *de gustibus non est disputandum*—in matters of taste there is no disputing. On this model, the expressive power of art signifies its capacity to enlarge our understanding of self, others, and the world. A landscape painting does not merely imitate the natural world nor does a portrait simply provide an accurate resemblance of its subject. We can assess landscape and portrait without direct acquaintance of the object. The truth value of a work of art is not determined by its mimetic representation of the world out there. Instead, we should better speak of learning something about the world and the human condition that is not captured otherwise than by a work of art. It is not wholly translatable into another medium of communication. The viewer, the listener, and the reader all must pay a disinterested attention to the work itself, not to what it represents or to the particular feelings that it arouses within us. The language of discovery is particularly apt and inescapable in at least some aesthetic judgements and commitments. Not all art may have this purpose and it may be none the worse for it— there is a place for the comical, the playful, and the fantastic. Yet some of what we consider great art—a Rembrandt self-portrait, Bach's Mass in B-Minor, a Donne sonnet—seems to demand appraisal in terms that do not reduce to neo-Darwinian categories. The language of disclosure, understanding, discovery, and vision, the sense of vocation that frequently accompanies artistic endeavour—all these presuppose a world that cannot be adequately described without recourse to aesthetic categories. What realists are inveighing against here is the claim that there might be a truly objective account of the world that does not reflect our distinctive perspective and human interests. It is as if the natural sciences might give us a robust description of the world, which then we would stain and gild with the colours of the mind whether these be moral, aesthetic, or religious. But such a bifurcation of fact and value does not reflect our discourse and thought. It is a fact of experience itself that from our perspective the world is irreducibly characterized by moral and aesthetic truths.

It has been argued against neo-Darwinian totalizing claims that the world as we know it and live in it requires the descriptive categories of art, morality, and religion. Explanation has different dimensions. It requires a stratified and multi-layered form if human concerns and experience are to be adequately expressed. The biological is necessary and important, but not exhaustive. These patterns of description are complementary and emergent in the history of the cosmos.[30] The relationship between them may be open and even interactive at times, but they do not function in competition with one another. Explanatory success in one domain does not in principle preclude the need for understanding in another. As Wentzel van Huyssteen argues, 'Shared rational resources may actually be identified for the very different cognitive domains of our lives precisely in the pragmatic performance of rationality in different reasoning strategies.'[31]

Nevertheless, there is a rejoinder that a secular critic might reasonably present. It goes like this. We can grant that a richer and more adequate account of human practice and forms of life requires that we recognize the non-reducible descriptions of art, religion, and morality. Yet, religion in important respects is the odd one out. All civilizations have their artistic traditions. But these can be recognized and appreciated without competition. An intermingling and cross-fertilizing of these can take place in ways that are creative and fruitful. Music and painting can bridge cultures rather than divide them. Ethics, moreover, is indispensable to any form of social organization. Different cultures have their varying standards and norms but we might hope to find a measure of commonality. The need to achieve some agreement and consensus on human rights and international law, for example, can be acknowledged by all people of good will. Furthermore, it might be said that we cannot conceive of a fulfilled life without ethical and artistic flourishing. These are human excellences that attach to any adequate account of living well. But can the same be said of religion? It may be possible to live well without it. Are not its outcomes typically divisive and destructive both for individual well-being and social harmony? Religious divisions have surely outlasted any social usefulness that they once had. And is it not inherently obstructive of human progress and development anyway because of the authoritative status assigned to ancient texts? Let us examine religion as it is actually believed and practised, the critic will say. A decent phenomenological description will reveal its shortcomings and why it is better to live without it, even though we cannot prosper without science, art, and morality. In the following chapters, we will examine more closely the historical record and attitudes of religious faith and practices.

Notes

1. Charles S. Peirce, *Collected Papers*, vol. vi: *Scientific Metaphysics* (Cambridge, MA: Harvard University Press, 1935), 311ff.
2. Some critics, most notably Plantinga, have sought to show that naturalism itself is internally inconsistent. While this may too readily convict the naturalist of logical incoherence, it does show the problems that a hard deterministic naturalism must encounter in evincing its own truthfulness. If we are determined

by the hard-wiring of our brain to think x, then we cannot also say with rational justification that x is true, only that we are predisposed to think it. This thought itself will then turn upon the theory that has spawned it with serpentine efficiency. If we are determined to be deterministic, then we have no compelling reasons for believing determinism to be true, or at least we cannot know that we have. See Alvin Plantinga, *Warrant and Proper Function* (New York: Oxford University Press, 1993), 216ff.

3. Jeffrey Stout, *Ethics After Babel* (Cambridge: Clarke, 1988), 214.

4. In much of what follows, I am indebted to the unpublished PhD thesis of Lisa M. D. Goddard, *An Interrogation of the Selfishness Paradigm in Sociobiology*, University of Chester, 2008.

5. The metaphor has been frequently challenged because of its apparent intentionality. Yet Dawkins notes that such metaphors have their uses in science and elsewhere.

6. W. D. Hamilton, 'The Genetical Evolution of Social Behaviour', *Journal of Theoretical Biology*, 7 (1964), 1–16, 17–52.

7. See Diane B. Paul, 'Darwin, Social Darwinism and Eugenics', in Jonathan Hodge (ed.), *The Cambridge Companion to Darwin* (Cambridge: Cambridge University Press, 2003), 214–39.

8. M. Daly and M. Wilson, *Homicide* (New York: De Gruyter, 1988).

9. See David Sloan Wilson, *Darwin's Cathedral: Evolution, Religion and the Nature of Society* (Chicago: University of Chicago Press, 2002), 13.

10. Ibid., 111.

11. Adam Smith, *An Inquiry into the Nature and Causes of The Wealth of Nations* (Oxford: Clarendon, 1976), 1.2.2, 26–7.

12. *Lectures on Jurisprudence*, (Oxford: Clarendon, 1978), 352.

13. David Hume, *An Enquiry concerning the Principles of Morals*, ed. L. A. Selby-Bigge, (Oxford: Clarendon, 1975), Appendix 1, 294. Taste does not concern truth and falsehood but rather 'has a productive faculty, and gilding or staining all natural objects with the colours, borrowed from internal sentiment raises in a manner a new creation.'

14. Edward O. Wilson and Michael Ruse, 'Moral Philosophy as Applied Science', *Philosophy*, 61 (1986), 173–92.

15. J. L. Mackie, *Ethics: Inventing Right and Wrong* (Harmondsworth: Penguin, 1977), 42.

16. I am indebted here to John Hare, 'Is There an Evolutionary Foundation for Human Morality?', in Philip Clayton and Jeffrey Schloss (eds.), *Evolution and Ethics: Human Morality in Biological and Religious Perspective* (Grand Rapids, MI: Eerdmans, 2004), 187–203.

17. Michael Ruse, *Taking Darwin Seriously* (Oxford: Blackwell, 1986), 253.

18. John Macmurray, *Persons in Relation* (London: Faber, 1961).

19. See Frans de Waal, *Primates and Philosophers: How Morality Evolved* (Princeton, NJ: Princeton University Press, 2006), 25ff.

20. Ibid., 34.

21. Peter Singer in de Waal, *Primates and Philosophers*, 146. For a significant account of how moral realism may be consistent with an evolutionary explanation of the origins of morality see Richard Joyce, *The Evolution of Morality* (Cambridge, MA: MIT Press, 2007).

22. Charles Darwin, *The Descent of Man* (London: Penguin, 2004), 115.

23. Stephen Pinker, *How the Mind Works* (London: Penguin, 1998), 521ff.

24. *Darwin's Cathedral*, 231.

25. Iris Murdoch, *The Fire and the Sun* (Oxford: Oxford University Press, 1977), 76–7.

26. Ibid., 78.

27. Ibid., 78.

28. Martin Heidegger, 'On the Origin of the Work of Art', in *Basic Writings*, ed. David Farrell Krell, 2nd edition (London: Routledge, 1993), 159. For further discussion see Fergus Kerr, *Immortal Longings: Versions of Transcending Humanity* (London: SPCK, 1997), 46ff.

29. For a robust defence of aesthetic cognitivism see Gordon Graham, *Philosophy of the Arts: An Introduction to Aesthetics*, 2nd edition (London: Routledge, 2000). In much of what follows, I draw upon his discussion.

30. Wentzel van Huyssteen has similarly argued for a transversal rationality that does not reduce all patterns of reasoning to one strategy but establishes common resources drawn from different domains. This is explored with reference *inter alia* to theology, anthropology, and palaeobiology in a discussion of human uniqueness. See *Alone in the World? Human Uniqueness in Science and Theology* (Grand Rapids, MI: Eerdmans, 2006).

31. Ibid., 12. There is a large body of literature on the different forms of emergentism. For a recent discussion of the issues in relation to religion see Niels Henrik Gregersen, 'Emergence: What is at Stake for Religious Reflection', in Philip Clayton and Paul Davies (eds.), *The Re-Emergence of Emergence: The Emergentist Hypothesis from Science to Religion* (Oxford: Oxford University Press, 2006), 279–302.

5

IS RELIGION BAD FOR OUR HEALTH? SAINTS, MARTYRS, AND TERRORISTS

In the preceding chapters, an open assessment of religious faith and practice has been urged. As a pervasive human activity, it has the capacity to enrich our understanding and experience of the world. Instead of a reductive explanation that accounts for it in terms of survival mechanisms, a more adequate description is required. This will take into account the ways in which religion is typically much more than a set of beliefs about the supernatural. For its practitioners, its forms of life determine their self-understanding, activity, and life-skills. Religion is about being and doing, as much as believing. However, a dominant feature of recent criticism of religion has been the ferocious attack on its outcomes. When studied close up, it is perceived as obscurantist, irrational, and with a propensity towards suppressing human freedom and promoting violence. Here again there is a departure from the old secularization thesis that tends to present faith as a picturesque phenomenon reflecting a private life-style choice. The recent resurgence of religion in global politics has drawn the fire of various critics, perhaps none more so than Christopher Hitchens who repeats the mantra that 'religion poisons everything'. While the baleful effects of religion have been noted in earlier periods, its resurgence in various conflict zones since the cold war has attracted widespread secular hostility today.

There is some tension here in the case against religion. As we have seen, the tendency of evolutionary psychology and sociobiology is to explain religion downwards. We are conditioned to think, act, and function religiously as a result of natural selection, adaptive strategies, and the drive to reproduce. In this respect, religion is the natural effect of something deeper and more primitive within human evolution. Alongside this, however, we are invited by the new atheism to see religion variously as the cause of disorder, violence, and abuse, and as the enemy of progress, reason, and enlightenment. Here the causal functions of religion seem to be underdetermined by the reductive accounts of its origin. To put the point more concretely, is it not more likely that the causes of violence between different ethnic groups have their roots in precisely those features of human nature that are also believed to determine religion? If the competition for survival is what produces religion, then can we blame religion for the competition? Dawkins concedes this point in noting that the tendencies towards in-group loyalties and out-group hostilities would exist in the absence of religion.[1] However, he claims that religion tends to exacerbate division in three ways—through the labelling of children, segregated schools, and taboos against 'marrying out'. This argument is at least coherent. There is a natural human tendency to favour in-groups and shun out-groups. Religion does not cause this, but it might significantly reinforce it. Whatever usefulness it might once have had, for societies that have a stake in pluralism and tolerance of difference religion may now be deleterious in its effects.

Several types of bad effect are identified by recent secular criticism. First, there is civil and international conflict. The religious roots of strife in Northern Ireland, Israel/Palestine, and the Balkans are all examined together with Islamist terrorism. In each of these, the presence of religious loyalties, convictions, and institutions is registered. Would it not be better if these societies were to become more secular, thus diminishing the ancient tribal loyalties that seem to be reinforced by the claims of each faith to be better and more truthful than its rivals? There must be something in this. For example, the secularization of the Irish republic and its stronger sense of a wider European identity have contributed something to the peace process in Northern Ireland. Anti-Catholic prejudice in Scotland has no doubt declined, though not disappeared, partly as a result of ceasing to project ourselves as a Protestant nation.[2] Religion plays little or no part in contemporary expressions of Scottish identity. The heroes of Scotland are no longer Columba, John Knox, David Livingstone, and Mary Slessor. They have been superseded, at least for the moment, by more secular figures such as William Wallace, Robert Burns, and Sean Connery. In part, this is a reaction caused by the perception that religion has been a divisive force in our past. For all their courage, the covenanters were not noted for tolerance and peaceful means of conflict resolution. Still less were their opponents. Indeed, while ideals of religious toleration were being advocated in England and elsewhere, they were strenuously resisted by Scottish divines in the mid seventeenth century. The recent scholarship of my colleague Jay Brown has also made us painfully aware of the hostile sectarianism that gripped sections of the Church of Scotland as recently as the 1920s when John White, minister of the Barony Church in Glasgow and leading figure in the General Assembly, denounced the menace of Irish Catholic immigration with its threat of pollution to the Scottish Protestant nation. While others opposed him and a younger generation ensured that energies were diverted in a more positive and ecumenical direction, the rhetoric and its popular appeal at that time remain chilling.[3]

If these vituperative sentiments have begun to disappear from our culture, this must have something to do with secularism. National identity in Scotland is nowhere defined religiously and the new parliament has taken much care to stress the plurality of citizens in modern Scottish society. Access to education, the professions, and public office is not conditioned by membership of any church or faith. There is a clearer differentiation of functions in political and civil society. The relative neutrality of the state with reference to faith groups is one of the key tenets of political liberalism and it is intended to ensure a greater degree of religious freedom than characterized the confessional states of Europe in the early seventeenth century. Thus secularization, defined in terms of differentiation rather than the sheer decline of religion, has something important to offer in combating the potentially toxic effects of religion. This ought to be recognized.

The extent to which faith is a cause of violent conflict is difficult to assess. There is a tendency in secular criticism of religion to move too swiftly from observing the faith commitments of extremists to asserting this as the single most relevant factor. On the other hand, there is also an opposing tendency amongst commentators too readily to discount the importance of religion. Ironically, this may itself be fuelled by secular incomprehension of religion, which assumes that it cannot be so important as to motivate people in this way. It simply masks an underlying cause such as poverty, lack of education, or loss of status. Alongside this, there may also be a propensity amongst exponents of toleration and pluralism to stress how the mainstream versions of each religious faith are essentially peaceful and cooperative in their outlook. These reactions were evident in the widespread discussion following 9/11.[4]

The role of the churches in various conflict zones has not been particularly noble. In the Balkans, Catholic and Orthodox loyalties fuelled long-standing enmities after the break-up of Yugoslavia. Following his capture, old TV footage of Radovan Karadzic has reminded us of the close proximity of Serbian

Orthodox leaders to his regime. Karadzic himself claimed that not a single decision was taken without the support of the church.[5] Instead of maintaining its distance from the civic authorities, the church acted primarily as an advocate of Serbian nationalism. Rwanda was one of the most Christian countries in sub-Saharan Africa, yet the presence of the churches did not prevent the worst genocide in recent history. The complexity of the conflict in Israel/Palestine is difficult to overestimate, yet again one cannot ignore the significance of religion and the intertwined histories of Judaism, Christianity, and Islam. These contribute powerfully and often negatively to the problems of the region, for example in virulently anti-Semitic rhetoric or in arguments that support the illegal occupation of Palestinian lands and the displacement of their inhabitants.

Northern Ireland provides a strong case for religion acting as a primary marker of sectarian identities. There religion has reinforced the segregation of communities and become embedded in the deep sectarian divide evident in education, housing, and patterns of marriage. Liechty and Clegg offer the following programmatic definition of 'sectarianism' which captures the integral role played by religion.

Sectarianism is a system of attitudes, actions, beliefs, and structures

- at personal, communal and institutional levels
- which always involves religion, and typically involves a negative mixing of religion and politics...which arises as a distorted expression of positive, human needs especially for belonging, identity, and the free expression of difference...and is expressed in destructive patterns of relating
- hardening the boundaries between groups
- overlooking others
- belittling, dehumanising, or demonising others
- justifying or collaborating in the domination of others
- physically or verbally intimidating or attacking others.[6]

While there is an array of causal factors—political, economic, historical, and social—religion cannot be detached from any of these. Interwoven in the fabric of sectarianism, it is unquestionably part of the problem. This incidentally should not surprise us if we understand how religion functions through ritual, custom, tradition, and communal identities. It is not to be identified merely with a set of irrational beliefs that can be isolated and then erased. In some respects, therefore, a better understanding of religion than we find in the new atheism may actually confirm the suspicion about its negative effects. To this extent, any exponent of religion will have to take very seriously its ambivalence as a social and political force, recognizing its capacity for entrenching out-group hostility.

Yet if there is to be a resolution of this problem it will need to come at least partly from within religious communities themselves. A programme that seeks to generate secession from faith to atheistic materialism is unlikely to provide the solution. What is required is a chastened understanding of religion by re-appropriation of internal resources that promote toleration and concord. And, despite the salience of religion in civil conflicts, a culture of peace-making at a grass-roots level can be discerned in Northern Ireland and elsewhere. Often these contribute to a climate in which peace, reconciliation, and a new politics become possible.[7] In Israel and Palestine, we have also to reckon with the presence of representatives of each of the Abrahamic faiths in initiatives to establish peace and justice.[8] The sociologist David Martin has argued that Christianity is most in danger of contributing to violence when it becomes too closely linked with the political state and national identity.[9] As a marker of such identity it can be a contributory factor to civil or international conflict. Yet in more differentiated societies where religion does not control or exercise a dominant influence upon political or civic life, it tends to function in a more authentic peace-making role. This, he argues, refutes the Dawkins thesis. When isolated from their wider host society religious groups tend to pacify rather than foment violence, unless these become too closely related to beleaguered ethnic

minorities. In this respect, Martin claims that the secularization of society has actually enabled the churches to retain a
more authentic expression of religion that comes closer to
what we find in the New Testament and the early church,
where no-one envisaged the spread or defence of the faith
by force.

Many of the responses to recent criticism of religion have
argued that atheist regimes have been culpable of repression,
brutality, and mass murder through much of the twentieth
century. In some respects, this is a distasteful debate. It is as
if we can settle the argument by ascertaining what has killed
more innocent people—religion or irreligion. Nevertheless,
there are issues here that require to be explored. In reading
Dawkins, Harris, or Hitchens one has the impression that
where religion is associated with brutality it tends to be isolated
as the salient causal element, whereas atheism is regarded in
contrasting cases merely as incidental—an inconsequential feature of political violence that requires to be explained in other
ways. For example, Harris suggests that the Hindu beliefs of
the Tamil Tiger terrorists have much to do with their commitment to suicide bombing despite the fact that this is largely
a secular movement with political ends.[10] Even more ten-
dentiously, Richard Dawkins writes 'Hitler and Stalin shared
atheism in common, they both also had moustaches, as does
Saddam Hussein. So what?'[11] This is hardly satisfactory. In the
case of communism, there are clear ideological links between
the rejection of religion and its suppression as a form of false
consciousness. This extends to other forms of dissidence and
provides the ideological veneer for violence on a massive scale.
The repression of communist regimes is apt to be forgotten or
lightly dismissed in the post-communist era, yet their persecution of those regarded as dissidents, revisionists, or enemies of
the state, including many religious believers, is staggering.

A further argument advanced by critics of religion focuses
on what Sam Harris calls 'the myth of moderation'. When

faced with the fact that many religious believers make for peaceful and law-abiding neighbours who are respectful of difference and freedoms, Harris and others suggest that their virtues are the result of having been infected by the values of secular liberalism. This has inoculated them against the intrinsic excesses of their faith and sacred scriptures. Such moderates are guilty of doublethink—they continue irrationally to adhere to ancient systems of superstition while manifesting those qualities that are expected of all citizens in a secular, democratic society. Without citing a single relevant source, Harris informs us that

The moderation we see among nonfundamentalists is not some sign that faith itself has evolved; it is, rather, the product of the many hammer blows of modernity that have exposed certain tenets of faith to doubt...Religious moderation is the product of *secular* knowledge and scriptural *ignorance*—and it has no bona fides, in religious terms, to put it on a par with fundamentalism.[12]

The preferred target of secular criticism is fundamentalism, which Harris describes inadequately as any literalist approach to sacred texts. This is viewed as the normative principle of all faiths from which moderation is adjudged a departure. Where this places long-standing and mainstream traditions of non-literal interpretation is another matter and one that we will discuss in the next chapter. But for the moment, it is sufficient to note that the improvement of religion is simply a sign for Harris that it has benefited from secular knowledge and enlightenment. As his argument unwinds, it quickly becomes clear that his real target is Islam. His discussion is governed by several principles as follows: Islam has never undergone an enlightenment analogous to that of Christianity and Judaism in Europe; its most sacred text commits it ineluctably to a violent politics that is not matched by the other Abrahamic faiths, although sections of the Pentateuch come close; what we call fundamentalist Islam or Islamism is the default setting of the religion; this point is missed by most secular liberals and politicians, who depict extremism as a deviation from a mainstream faith that is essentially noble and peaceful; the future security and well-being of the world depend upon naming and challenging Islam, and requiring it to undergo a process of secular enlightenment. While religion is the generic enemy, its most potent and deadly species is Islam, according to this critique.

Harris's argument has a veneer of plausibility. He cites at great length passages from the Qur'an that appear to incite violence towards infidels, apostates, and heretics while offering eternal rewards for those who heed these injunctions. Repeatedly, he insists that if you really believe those things then they must make a radical difference to the ways you think and act. These are powerful levers; when pulled they can have devastating effects. Huntingdon's thesis about the 'clash of civilizations' becomes a simpler and more jarring 'clash of ideologies' in Harris's scenario. A direct and quite simple causal connection is established between sacred text and suicide bombings. Other explanations such as poverty or lack of education are set aside—many terrorists are highly educated and affluent. The only explanation must be an irrational and pathological set of religious beliefs. However, this requires some patient analysis, rather than a knee-jerk response.

The notion of martyrdom has had a long and varied history in religious and secular traditions. A willingness to die in the service of God and the keeping of one's faith is evident throughout much of the Hebrew Scriptures. It was a way of honouring God and maintaining the cause of God's people, as in the examples of Daniel and the three men in the fiery furnace. In the inter-testamental period, the example of the Maccabean martyrs extends this further. In some cases, these are soldiers willing to sacrifice their lives whether by submitting to death at the hands of the enemy or else by committing suicide as a heroic avoidance of apostasy or capture by the enemy. Such is the account that Josephus offers of the mass suicide at Masada. What is notable in the literature is the added sense of privilege and ecstasy in making the highest sacrifice before God. Stories are found in Jewish literature of mothers urging their children to hold fast to their faith to the point of death. An eternal reward is now offered and acts as an incentive for selfless action. So a tradition of martyrdom develops with these identifying marks: keeping one's faith in the face of a mortal threat; the honour attaching to the supreme sacrifice; its beneficial effects for the subsequent history of the faith community; and the prospect of divine justice and eschatological fulfilment.

Socrates, Jesus, and Muhammad provide contrasting examples of bearing witness for their faith.[13] Suffering an agonizing death by violent crucifixion, Jesus goes to his death willingly but passively. While there are analogies that were exploited in the arguments of early Christian apologists, the death of Jesus is more harrowing than the calm and serene passing of Socrates as he drinks the hemlock. Both, however, seem to anticipate a future vindication. For Jesus and Socrates, there is no violent resistance, an example followed in the early centuries of Christianity. Neither do they in the end seek to avoid death but meet it willingly. Both die as victims of political and religious collaboration but not in a military struggle. Moreover, each dies alone; he does not take his friends down with him. This contrasts with the heroism of Odysseus in Homer's epic poem where all of his companions perish on the return journey from the Trojan wars. Odysseus alone makes it back to Ithaca and to the waiting Penelope. Jesus, by contrast, dies but is able to spare his followers, even if many of them were later to suffer martyrdom in his cause.

Dying for one's faith is celebrated amongst early Christian writers, most famously by Tertullian in his remark about their blood being the seed of the faith. Their example is recorded and is instrumental in bringing others into the church. Lists of martyrs are compiled, their stories being recounted and celebrated on special feast days. The bonds that maintain the church are even more powerful than those of family, kin, and the love of life. At the same time, however, there emerges a more cautious approach to martyrdom in other early Christian writers. Whether this is through political compromise or theological discernment can be debated. Yet what we find emerging are criteria that are to be employed by Christians to determine a proportionate response in circumstances of conflict. While one is never to deny the faith, a martyr's death is not actively to be sought. Clement, for example, argues that one should take reasonable steps to protect oneself. Only thus can one hear the genuine call of God to sacrifice one's own life. In such cases, the action ceases to be described as suicide and instead becomes martyrdom.[14]

The example of Muhammad is different in important respects. To defend his faith and his community, he wages war against his aggressors. In 622, at the start of the Muslim era, he is called to the path of active resistance. The community in Medina fought over sixty battles against rival forces, Muhammad participating in twenty-seven of these. The most memorable was the battle at the oasis of Badr in 624 and the celebrated words of Khubaib al-Ansari when captured and sold. 'It does not matter when or how I am killed as a Muslim as long as my death is for the sake of Allah.'[15] The improbable victory of Muhammad at Badr was a sign of divine favour, and a vindication of jihad. The subsequent history of Islam was of course marked by rapid expansion and territorial conquest, first of the Arab heartland and then later, by 750, of a much wider region stretching from Afghanistan in the north-east to Spain and North Africa in the west. This led to patterns of co-existence or *convivencia* with Jews and Christians who enjoyed a degree of protection subject to payment of taxes. The text of the Qur'an, moreover, does not generally favour wars of aggression. The power of the sword was to be used vigorously but defensively. 'Those who have been attacked are

permitted to take up arms because they have been wronged—
God has the power to help them—those who have been driven
unjustly from their homes for saying, "Our Lord is God"'
(Surah 22: 39–40). The following verse, moreover, speaks
about the need to defend not just mosques but monaster-
ies, churches, and synagogues where God's name is invoked
and which are threatened with destruction. Elsewhere in the
Qur'an their position is compared to that of the Israelites
as oppressed by the Egyptians. This duty of resistance is
demanded of believers and the rewards of paradise await them
when they prove themselves faithful. 'God will not let the
deeds of those who are killed for His cause come to nothing'
(Surah 47: 4).

Similar reflections about the legitimacy and necessity of
waging war can be found in sections of the Hebrew Bible, particularly in the stories of the conquest that follow the exodus
from Egypt. Many of these passages are highly problematic for
later traditions of interpretation, and still today for Palestinian
Christians. We might also note that the tradition of the just
war that emerges in Augustine and other Christian writers sets
out rather similar criteria to those suggested by the Qur'an
for the waging of war by the state, though not by the church.
The spirit of jihad, moreover, had shifted by the middle of the
eighth century as Islamic civilization flourished and peaceful
co-existence with neighbours was achieved. No doubt it is easy
to idealize the nature and extent of co-existence throughout
this period, but it is certainly not marked by extensive wars
or genocidal persecution. At the very least, this should caution
against the simplistic assumption (as in Harris) that the standard mode of Islamic engagement with the non-Muslim world
is one of violent conflict.

The recent phenomenon of 'predatory martyrdom'[16] represents a grotesque mutation of a long tradition of martyrdom in
religious and secular politics. Foreshadowed by the kamikaze
campaigns of Japanese pilots in the final phase of the second

world war, it involves the suicide of the martyr as a military action in which enemy lives are also taken. In the case of recent predatory martyrdom, however, this is usually an indiscriminate attack on anyone in the target zone, whether these are soldiers, civilians, children, sick or disabled persons. The most dramatic and highly publicized was of course the 9/11 attack on the twin towers of New York which took more lives in one hour than the bombing of Pearl Harbour or all the troubles in Northern Ireland. This cult of predatory martyrdom can be more immediately traced back to the 1983 campaigns of Hezbollah on the US embassy in Beirut and on American and French barracks. Vowing revenge on the organization, President Reagan's comments had the effect of raising the profile of suicide bombers internationally. The most sustained adoption of this tactic was by the Liberation Tigers of Tamil Eelam, otherwise known as the Tamil Tigers. Largely secular in its outlook, it harnessed religious images of martyrdom to encourage and valorize those who participated in suicide attacks. Women and children were recruited to this end, the most publicized attack being that of a young woman, Dhanu, on Rajiv Gandhi in July 1985. Wearing a pregnancy smock, she concealed a large explosive device around her stomach. A garland of flowers was held in one hand and a triggering device in the other. After kissing Gandhi's feet, the bomb was detonated. killing a total of eighteen people including Dhanu and her prime target.

In his recent study of suicide bombings, Farhad Khosrokhavar has pointed to the range of contexts in which these have taken place in recent times.[17] A social scientist working in Paris, Khosrokhavar conducted a series of interviews from the 1990s onwards with jailed militants in different parts of the world. His conclusion is that the different motives and settings for suicide bombing are concealed by use of a common Muslim discourse of jihad and martyrdom. In particular, he distinguishes two types of context with varying sets of causes. The first and classic case is that of those engaged in a process of nation-building. Perceiving the cause to be almost impossible they embrace suicide either to assist others after their death or simply to wreak vengeance on their enemies. Examples from Iran, Algeria, Lebanon, and Palestine all illustrate this more familiar cause of terrorism—the desire for independence, national recognition, and freedom from a perceived foreign tyranny. More recently, a similar set of causes has emerged following the collapse of the Soviet Union. Nation-building in Chechnya requires a bloody struggle against Russian supremacy, but with clear political ends.

Contrast this with the ideology of Al-Qaeda and its brand of global terrorism, which renders any western city a potential target whether New York, Madrid, London, or Glasgow. Here there is no overriding commitment to a single political collective or local cause. It is a movement that rejects the spread of a global culture—its cities are rootless and godless places in which to live; its political might has oppressed the heartlands of Islam in the middle east; and its client state Israel, a small nation, has humiliated its larger neighbours and displaced an indigenous Muslim population. Moreover, the terror of this movement is largely nihilistic. A protest movement, it represents a violent counter-reaction without any clear political goals except perhaps to usher in some apocalyptic scenario that offers judgement upon the world and vindication to the faithful.[18] Khosrokhavar notes not only the hopelessness of this movement but also the irony of its location. It is itself a product of western, globalized culture. Its exponents are familiar with our affluent cities. Often they are themselves educated, professional, and wealthy. They can deploy cyberspace and the latest technology to devastating effect. As Muslims, they represent only a tiny minority, albeit an active and dangerous one. Despite the threat of this grouping, Khosrokhavar remains hopeful of the emergence of a new generation of Muslim intellectuals capable of interpreting texts and traditions in ways that can advance democracy, alongside other groups who can espouse customs of modern life while retaining their Islamic identity. The only way forward is the nurture of such groups and the patient removal of the grievances that drive others to violence.

One of the key issues confronting Muslim intellectuals today is how to interpret the relationship of the state to the religious community in a pluralist society. This has been pressed explicitly by Benedict XVI in a pre-Christmas address in 2006.

One must welcome the true conquests of the Enlightenment, human rights and especially the freedom of faith and its practice, and recognize these also as being essential elements for the authenticity of religion...As in the Christian community, where there has been a long search to find the correct position of faith in relation to such beliefs—a search that will certainly never be concluded once and for all—so also the Islamic world with its own tradition faces the immense task of finding the appropriate solutions in this regard.[19]

However, some important Muslim responses to this issue are already out there in the public domain. Tariq Ramadan, for example, in discussing the traditional dichotomy between the *dar al-islam* (the abode of Islam) and the *dar al-harb* (the abode of war), has suggested that the situation in which western Muslims find themselves corresponds to neither of these categories. It is a context in which the freedom to practise their faith is available as also a freedom to bear witness in constructive ways to that faith before the rest of civil society. This situation is more akin to a *dar al-dawa* (the abode of invitation to God). This indeed is redolent of the context in which Muhammad and his followers found themselves in Mecca prior to their Hijra to Medina. In a minority, they had a responsibility to attest their faith before their people. Ramadan writes,

[W]herever a Muslim who declares 'I bear witness that there is no god but God and Muhammad is His messenger' lives in security and can fulfil his fundamental religious obligations, he is at home, for the

Prophet taught us that the whole world is a mosque. This means that Muslims living in the West, individuals as well as communities from various countries, not only may live there but are also the bearers of an enormous responsibility: they must give their society a testimony based on faith, spirituality, values, a sense of where boundaries lie, and a permanent human and social engagement.[20]

John Esposito points out that the concept of 'jihad' can be constructed in multiple ways.[21] There is no single doctrine that has commanded universal support or has broad institutional sanction. Contrasting positions are determined by the interpretation and application of sacred texts in different historical and political contexts. This differentiated approach is already present in the life of Muhammad as he migrates from Mecca to Medina and becomes engaged in a defensive jihad against warring opponents. Contemporary voices of Islam offer at least four different interpretations of the nature of jihad: leading a devout and disciplined Muslim life committed to one's family and faith; working for the spread of Islam; supporting the struggle of oppressed Muslim peoples in Palestine, Chechnya, or Kosovo; or, in the case of Osama bin Laden and his followers, working to overthrow governments in the middle east and attacking America. Each interpretation has a complex cultural and historical location. To understand the last of these, for example, one needs to learn about the colonial occupation of the middle east and Africa from the eighteenth century, the rise of Islamic reform movements, the historical influence of figures such as Abd al-Wahhab in Saudi Arabia and Sayyid Qutb in Egypt, their criticism of corrupt regimes, the failure of secular nationalism, the humiliation of the 1967 war, the displacement of Palestinian peoples, the hegemony of global capitalism with the transmission of messages and values from the affluent west, and so on. While contested interpretations of sacred texts are always present, there is no straight line from the Qur'an to bin Laden. There is neither one single mode of engagement with non-Muslim peoples nor an egregious tendency towards violence. The historical evidence coupled with today's geographical differences indicates something more multifarious.

In grappling with these issues, western scholars and commentators have often considered the legacy of the crusades from the late eleventh century, when Christian forces were encouraged to recover and retain the Holy Land from Islam. Today repentance and recantation on the part of Christians have become the norm. The violence, abuse, and enmity provoked are now deplored. The religious sanction of these military expeditions, the indulgences offered to warrior saints, and the theological legitimization of their work are all deplored. Christian groups have sought to offer public apology in different ways to Muslims and Jews.

The treatment of the crusades sometimes presents this as an aberration from a religion that is essentially pacifist. Yet the problems for Christianity and its relationship to Islam may run deeper.[22] The crusades lasted many centuries and were conducted in several theatres of war, not only in the middle east but in Europe and North Africa. The enemies against whom armies crusaded were not only Muslims but included pagans and orthodox Christian groups. Moreover, the culture of the crusades spawned internal violence and repression within Christian societies, this being directed towards Jews and heretics. The theologians of the middle ages and the Reformation generally supported the use of force to suppress heresy and dissent. What this suggests is that warfare is deeply embedded in much of church history as a mechanism for the extension of Christ's kingdom. While the just war tradition specifies that force may be a last resort, a lesser evil required on occasion to offset a much greater evil, the history of the tradition reveals how deeply complicit the church was in most of the wars that were waged by European empires, states, and confederations. From a Muslim perspective, the crusades symptomize more than an isolated episode that can be viewed as a departure from standard practice. Instead this is often perceived as part of a long history of hostility and aggression that now takes the form of cultural and economic colonization. One western Muslim has written,

The memory of the crusades lingers in the Middle East and colours Muslim perceptions of Europe. It is the memory of an aggressive, backward and religiously fanatic Europe. This historical memory would be reinforced in the nineteenth and twentieth centuries as imperial Europeans once again arrived to subjugate and colonize territories in the Middle East. Unfortunately this legacy of bitterness is overlooked by most Europeans when thinking of the Crusades.[23]

Where does this leave us? The argument now appears to have turned direction to confirm the worst misgivings of secular critics about the inherent tendency of religions towards the justification of violence. This monolithic judgement is an overstatement, but it does point to what Appleby calls 'the ambivalence of the sacred'. Undoubtedly, there are ways in which religion has historically lent its support to war. In different ways, it has fuelled grievances, defined and entrenched conflictual identities, provided incentives to violence, and promised vindication and reward to those charged with waging war. These are more extensive than believers might wish to recognize and require careful self-examination on the part of faith communities.

On the other hand, one can also find a corresponding contribution of religion to the flourishing of civilizations, their cultural achievements, and the peaceful co-existence of peoples of different race, language, and religion. The term 'medieval' is often used carelessly as a synonym for 'irrational', 'bigoted', and 'out-of-date'. Attitudes in the dark ages are compared unfavourably with the more enlightened views of modernity. Protestantism may have something to do with this reading of the middle ages. The time warp that it imposed upon the theological curriculum suggested that pretty much nothing of value happened between the middle of the fifth century and the eve of the Reformation. Yet this is a serious distortion that ignores the flourishing of Islamic civilization as well as the rich intellectual debates that took place amongst Jewish, Christian, and Muslim philosophers of the time. The great centres of *convivencia*—in Cordoba, Toledo, Palermo, and Constantinople, for example—testify to the long periods of co-existence of Jews, Christians, and Muslims resulting in significant economic, scientific, and artistic advance. While this period is flanked by epochal battles and the misery inflicted by the crusades, it points to the capacity of faiths to live together peaceably.[24]

It is tempting here to say merely that human nature has a deep-seated ability for good and evil in almost equal admixture, and that religion can be annexed to either propensity. But more attention needs to be given to the conditions which tend to manifest one tendency rather than another. Under what circumstances do religions find themselves colluding in or even advocating war? David Martin, in his aforementioned study, claims that the causes of war are often multiple and that religion is at most one factor amongst many, functioning as a contingent marker of identity.[25] Other causes are generally present. Typically these include ethnicity, a struggle for power, oppression, historical grievances, poverty, and inequality. Moreover, where there arises a differentiation of functions within a society, religion ceases to be a strong marker of a collective civic identity and is therefore better placed to act critically and to exercise a constraining effect upon political excesses. Martin also notes that in conflict zones where religion is not a factor (e.g. North Korea), the potential for violence is undiminished. A recent study commissioned by the BBC from scholars at the Institute for Peace Studies in Bradford argues that the relationship of religion to war needs to be assessed in terms of mobilization, discourse, and purpose. Their broad-brush conclusion based on existing research is that while some wars can be registered as profoundly religious—the crusades, wars of Arab expansion, the confessional wars in Reformation and early modern Europe—most wars that have been fought in the twentieth century cannot be regarded as 'genuinely religious'.[26] Moreover, the mass murders that took place in Nazi Germany, the Soviet Union, and the People's Republic of China in the time of Hitler, Stalin, and Mao, accounting for around 75 per cent of all killings last century, cannot be attributed to the violent effects of religion.

The Soviet Union provides clear evidence for the effect of a Marxist-Leninist ideology of atheism on religious practice, association, and representation.[27] From 1917 onwards, there was a concerted attempt to suppress religion through the confiscating of church properties, the curtailment of religious practice (including charitable activities), and the destruction of the church hierarchy. Consequently, many leaders in the Russian Orthodox Church suffered prolonged imprisonment or were forced into exile. Undoubtedly, attitudes to the national church were relaxed during the Second World War when its mobilizing function was recognized as important for national morale. Yet a further onslaught took place in 1959–64, during the Khrushchev years, when earlier repressive measures returned. To deny that this persecution of religion was connected to the official atheism of the regime is simply to ignore the evidence.

One of the significant trends identified in such studies is the extent to which conflict is intensified by the deployment of religious images and rituals. It is used to valorize a political cause and thus to mobilize support whether through political rhetoric, the bestowal of martyrdom upon the war dead, or the use of symbol and ritual to articulate and sanctify the movement. The Italian political philosopher Emilio Gentile has shown that this is a pervasive feature of several twentieth-century movements, including fascism, Nazism, and communism, and continues to be expressed in a good deal of civil religion. Quoting Saint-Simon's remark that religion cannot disappear from the world but only transform itself, Gentile argues that traditional expressions of religion are typically usurped rather than annihilated by new forms of politics.[28]

At the same time, it should be remembered that the vast bulk of the adherents of all the world's religions make civil and law-abiding neighbours. By their own testimony, their faith makes them more peaceable than they would otherwise be. This is not to underestimate the capacity of religion for pathological hatred and intolerance but it is to seek a more balanced reading of its record. If the New Testament is to be believed, the saints are not paragons of virtue who have no need of forgiveness, but they are people who testify to a faith that has made them better than they would otherwise be. Their faith is not demonstrable or without its flaws. For others, there may be different ways of living well. Yet their testimony is genuine and merits proper attention. A fair hearing was what the early exponents of Christian faith requested of their pagan audiences and this ought still to be accorded people of good faith everywhere.

The practical effects of faith on the lives of individuals and communities is difficult to quantify and often falls below the radar screen of historical interpretation. Yet consider this passage from Herbert Butterfield's *Christianity and History*, written almost sixty years ago.

Even serious students ... have tended to overlook that more intimate thing, the inner spiritual life of the Church. The ordinary historian, when he comes, shall we say, to the year 1800 does not think to point out to his readers that in this year, still, as in so many previous years, thousands and thousands of priests and ministers were preaching the Gospel week in and week out, constantly reminding the farmer and the shopkeeper of charity and humility, persuading them to think for a moment about the great issues of life, and inducing them to confess their sins. Yet this was a phenomenon calculated greatly to alter the quality of life and the very texture of human history; and it has been the standing work of the Church throughout the ages.[29]

Part of the problem may be that good news is no news. It is only the abuses of religion that command the headlines. Much of the patient, constructive, and mundane work of the churches and other faith groups proceeds day by day without media comment. *Salt of the Earth*, a recent intensive study of the civic contribution of churches in Glasgow revealed that in 2006 there were 315 churches in the city which generated 2,382 activities, including support groups, counselling, social justice work, groups supporting the creative arts, and health, fitness, and education classes.[30] A disproportionately high number of these churches are located in the more deprived areas of the city. Essential support is also offered to uniformed organizations, while there are almost 2,000 separate fund-raising ventures. Much of the work, over one-half, was directed towards community involvement rather than to the internal life of the congregations themselves. In the course of each week, over 57,000 people within the city were estimated to participate in one or more of these activities, providing a total of more than 2.5 million annual attendances. These are not headline-grabbing statistics, but they require to be taken into account in any audit of the beneficial outcomes of faith for individuals and communities.

A further type of bad effect identified by recent criticism of religion is resistance to secular progress, particularly in the realm of health care. Hitchens cites examples of religious communities resisting vaccination programmes, refusing to admit the benefits of condoms as a barrier to infection, failing to protect children in their care, mutilating women through the ritual of female circumcision, and generally producing guilt-ridden attitudes towards sex. Again it has to be said that the list of charges is impressive and even salutary. On much of this, he is simply right. The churches and other faith groups have sometimes been the obstacles to progress and have had to be led by secular trends on a raft of issues—gender equality, democracy, artificial contraception, divorce, and human rights. But again a more balanced account must acknowledge the historic role of faith communities in providing education, medical care, and poor relief. For many centuries, the churches were the main suppliers of these public benefits and only recently has the state ensured more comprehensive provision. Similarly, missionary expansion in Asia, Africa, and Latin America was generally accompanied by a contribution to education and health care on the part of the churches. This continues to be the case and the contribution to civil well-being and social capital by faith communities has been the focus of renewed attention by social scientists in different parts of the world. In the particular case of the social democracies of Europe, the churches in the post-war period have generally supported and facilitated the systematic state provision of medicine, education, and welfare. They have been part of this project, rather than amongst its detractors. This incidentally is why the social theologies of the mainstream churches have generally been to the left of all our governments since Mrs Thatcher became Prime Minister in 1979. Yet there are only the merest hints of all this in the writings of the new atheists.[31] And in Islamic societies, again it is often faith-based political groups that provide schools, medical support, and relief in the absence of state provision.

Research indicates that the practice of faith is generally good for one's psychological and social well-being. For example a survey in the USA in 2002 of almost 500 studies in scholarly journals concludes that there is a clear correlation between religious commitment and higher levels of well-being and self-esteem, and also lower levels of hypertension, depression, and criminal activity.[32] Other research suggests that religious people live longer and healthier lives, with lower levels of drug and alcohol abuse and criminal delinquency. This evidence should not be over-played. Faith does not present itself primarily as a strategy for long life, health, and prosperity even if significant sections of Christianity have fallen into that trap. The early Christians would have been surprised if longevity had been presented as an inducement for believing; many of them did not expect to live long or comfortable lives. The logic of faith is that one must lose one's life in order to find it. The benefits that accrue to the individual do so indirectly by a focus and reorientation of the self upon a set of goals and commitments that are not inherently inward-looking. In any case, physical and psychological well-being, we are informed, may also be promoted by a range of other activities such as choral singing, country dancing, and golfing. But what the research does emphatically show is that those who practise faith are typically not violent, delusionary, authoritarian, naïve, and fanatical—all of which might be predicted if the hysterical claims of some critics were credible.

Finally, what about the children? A repeated charge is that religions are guilty of child abuse by virtue of their indoctrination of youngsters and the servile habits they inculcate. We can again find examples that appear to confirm this, for example the grisly stories recounted by Dawkins of children being subjected to movies about the likely conditions of hell in order to constrain their behaviour. However, once again the pathological examples that are adduced do not confirm the hypothesis that religious nurture amounts to brainwashing, let alone abuse. The forms of Christian education with which we are familiar in our churches and schools often enable youngsters to develop skills of discernment and interpretation. They are given freedom and encouragement to make responsible decisions for themselves as they reach adulthood. If there is any brainwashing in our culture then it is surely the sort that derives from peer-group pressure and the media. These function far more powerfully in the consciousness of children and teenagers than do the strictures of their Sunday School teachers.

There is something chilling in the suggestion that we should find ways of preventing parents enculturating their children in the tradition, practices, and beliefs that they hold most precious.[33] Who is to determine the appropriate boundaries, standards, and sanctions? Do we want to outlaw some ways of life such as that of the Amish? In any case, some experience of religion should not be excluded from childhood. It has been part of human experience for thousands of years, and some exposure is required to ensure later discrimination and meaningful choice. Even Dawkins has spoken of the pleasure he derives from carol services at Christmas time. In any case, as we have seen, religion is not reducible to a discrete set of beliefs. It is bound up with traditions of dress, clothing, music, festival, and family celebrations. The maintenance of ethnic identity is closely tied to religious tradition. To insulate children from this is neither possible nor profitable. There is no form of upbringing that can represent a view from nowhere. Every child requires to be immersed in some cultural traditions and their accompanying forms of training and development.

John Stuart Mill's private education in the mid-nineteenth century provides the mirror image of this. Taught from the earliest age by his father to work things out for himself, he was nevertheless left in no doubt as to the force of his father's agnosticism. 'He impressed upon me from the first, that the manner in which the world came into existence was a subject on which nothing was known.'[34] Mill then goes on to note that he was one of the very few examples in Britain at that time of someone who never had religious belief in the first place and thus had nothing to discard. It seems that there is no education or upbringing that does not leave the imprint of training, nurture, and context.

The unbalanced attack on religion by much of the new atheism makes us instinctively hostile in our response. However, what is needed is a more measured and considered debate. Not all their criticisms are misplaced. We need to recognize the inherent dangers of some mutations of religion, the presence of superstitious elements in much popular piety, and the need for a critical and informed account of our religion. One's own faith will be chastened and even enriched in this encounter. Somewhat whimsically, the Chief Rabbi has raised the question, 'why did God create atheists?'[35] His answer is that we need them to understand ourselves, our faith, and our world better. We need to be intellectually and morally braced by such criticism—it might save us from sloppy thinking, from easy deception and sheltering behind notions that do not withstand critical inspection.

Sacks makes the interesting point that the faithful are sometimes guilty of believing too much. We believe that suffering is sent by God to punish or test us, or that it is right to coerce people into believing, or that we should not tolerate those who think and act differently from ourselves. Some beliefs that ought to be matters of relative indifference are exalted into causes for schism and division. Atheism can confront and challenge this excess of belief, the false zeal that characterizes expressions of faith everywhere. For evidence of such excess, simply check any recent blog on a religious news story.

The Dawkins-led onslaught on religion tends to construe all believers as either fools or knaves or both. The more reflective versions of faith that flourish in all traditions tend to be marginalized as unimportant or hopelessly compromised. We should not allow this. Christianity is always adapting itself into something that can be believed. While it has core elements and themes, the faith delivered once for all to the saints has to be restated and rethought in every generation. We should not be reluctant or unwilling to undertake this task, particularly in relation to other religions and the natural sciences. Faith itself must be allowed to evolve. Ironically, while Dawkins embraces enthusiastically the development and shifting of moral beliefs, he will not concede such a process of evolution to faith communities. Patient dialogue is eschewed in favour of a 'winner takes all' contest.

Much of the current debate tends to be preoccupied for obvious reasons with Islam, but it too has its calm and constructive voices and those who believe that it can flourish in a constructive and conciliatory way in European societies. This happened for much of the middle ages with patterns of *convivencia*, or co-existence, and we will have to learn this again. This is a task for Christians, Muslims, and humanists. If we want to defend Christianity from easy caricatures and to present its moderate and progressive side, then we should allow Muslim apologists to do the same for their faith. For this reason amongst others, education remains a vital component of all faith traditions. Institutions of education need to flourish within and alongside faith communities. They have a critical, reflective, and constructive contribution to make to the self-interpretation of faith in changing social and intellectual circumstances. This is why incidentally it would be disastrous at this moment in our history for the study of theology and religion to be removed from our universities. Academic study needs to flourish at a distance that results neither in slavish adherence to religious bodies nor in a disdainful and supercilious scepticism. Empathetic and constructive criticism is required and universities continue to offer the best space currently available for this task, especially in the UK where the study of theology is closely tied in the syllabus to social-scientific approaches to religion.[36]

One of the ironies of the new atheism is that it arouses the very kind of divisiveness and hostility that it attributes uniquely to the power of religion. This has been challenged by other secular humanists who wisely argue that the messy business of democratic politics requires making common cause, building alliances, and seeking compromises amidst sharp disagreement. The future of the human race and the planet's ecosystem requires the cooperation of people of all faiths and none. Humanists need to be part of this broad coalition and to exercise a positive contribution. The major world religions command greater support than ever before; only in western Europe have we seen very significant decline. A broader, global perspective is required to discern the importance of bridge-building and gathering of support across boundaries. Strategies need to be identified and owned by traditions of wisdom that can be found across cultures and religions. Bernard Crick, a leading political philosopher, has complained about the counter-productive effects of the savage and intolerant attacks of his fellow humanists. What is needed is the forging of alliances with faith-based groups that are better able to challenge and amend the ways of their co-religionists by mustering theological and textual arguments for their position. He quotes the celebrated story of Voltaire on his deathbed. When exhorted by a priest to renounce the devil and all his ways, Voltaire replied that it was not a time for making enemies. So also the political goals of humanism are not advanced by making enemies of all believers, according to Crick. 'Fundamentalism and fanaticism are rife, but are being rejected or resisted within their own religions by most Christians and Muslims. If we humanists are fully secure in our non-belief, scepticism, and secularism, we can work together with those of all beliefs who fight against new or born-again enemies to freedom.'[37] Atheism too has its moderate and patient voices. Believers should welcome that fact, learn from there, and make common cause where they can.

Notes

1. Richard Dawkins, *The God Delusion*, 260.
2. See Tom Devine, *Scotland's Shame: Bigotry and Sectarianism in Modern Scotland* (Edinburgh: Mainstream, 2000).
3. See Stewart J. Brown, 'Presbyterians and Catholics in Twentieth-Century Scotland', in Stewart J. Brown and George Newlands (eds.), *Scottish Christianity in the Modern World* (Edinburgh: T&T Clark, 2000), 255–82.
4. This is effectively explored by Oliver McTernan, *Violence in God's Name: Religion in an Age of Conflict* (London: Darton, Longman & Todd, 2003), 20ff.
5. Paul Mojzes, *Religion and the War in Bosnia* (Atlanta: Scholars Press, 1998), 89.
6. Joseph Liechty and Cecilia Clegg, *Moving Beyond Sectarianism: Religion, Conflict and Reconciliation in Northern Ireland* (Dublin: Columba Press, 2001), 102–3.
7. Perhaps the best recent explorations of this is R. Scott Appleby, *The Ambivalence of the Sacred: Religion, Violence and Reconciliation* (New York: Rowman & Littlefield, 2000).
8. See for example Maureen and Robin Tobin (eds.), *How Long O Lord? Christian, Jewish and Muslim Voices from the Ground and Visions for the Future* (Cambridge, MA: Cowley, 2002).
9. David Martin, *Does Christianity Cause War?* (Oxford: Oxford University Press, 1997).
10. Sam Harris, *The End of Faith: Religion, Terror, and the Future of Reason* (Norton: New York, 2004), 239.
11. *The God Delusion*, 273.
12. Sam Harris, *The End of Faith*, 19 and 21.
13. For a brief history of martyrdom in the ancient and modern world see Hugh Barlow, *Dead for Good: Martyrdom and the Rise of the Suicide Bomber* (London: Paradigm, 2007).
14. For a recent study of attitudes and practice in the early church see Paul Middleton, *Radical Martyrdom and Cosmic Conflict in Early Christianity* (London: T&T Clark, 2006).
15. Cited by Barlow, *Dead for Good*, 52.
16. The phrase is borrowed from Barlow, *Dead for Good*, 130.
17. Farhad Khosrokhavar, *Suicide Bombers: Allah's New Martyrs* (London: Pluto, 2005).

18. Nonetheless, Osama bin Laden himself is deeply committed to the overthrow of the Saudi government and to the restoration of the Caliphate.

19. As cited in http://www.vatican.va/holy_father/benedict_xvi/speeches/2006/december/.

20. Tariq Ramadan, *Western Muslims and the Future of Islam* (Oxford: Oxford University Press, 2004), 72–3.

21. John Esposito, *Unholy War* (Oxford: Oxford University Press, 2002), 26ff.

22. See the argument of Jonathan Riley-Smith, 'Rethinking the Crusades', *First Things* (March 2000), 20–3 and also his discussion in *What Were the Crusades?*, 3rd edition (London: Palgrave Macmillan, 2002).

23. Akbar S. Ahmed, *Living Islam: From Samarkand to Stornoway* (London: BBC, 1993), 76. I owe this reference to Carole Hillenbrand's important study *The Crusades: Islamic Perspectives* (Edinburgh: Edinburgh University Press, 1999), 590.

24. See for example Stephen O'Shea, *Sea of Faith: Islam and Christianity in the Medieval Mediterranean World* (London: Profile, 2006).

25. David Martin, *Does Christianity Cause War?* For discussion of Martin's thesis see Keith Ward, *Is Religion Dangerous?* (London: Lion Hudson, 2006), 77ff. An overview of the wider issues is offered by Alister McGrath with Joanna Collicut, *The Dawkins Delusion? Atheist Fundamentalism and the Denial of the Divine* (London: SPCK, 2007), 46ff.

26. Greg Austin, Todd Kranock, and Thom Oommen, 'God and War: An Audit & Explanation' at http://news.bbc.co.uk/1/shared/spl/hi/world/04/war_audit_pdf/pdf/war_audit.pdf. For further discussion of this work see Tina Beattie, *The New Atheists* (London: Darton, Longman & Todd, 2007), 78ff.

27. See for example Alexander A. Bogolepov, 'Legal Position of the Russian Orthodox Church in the Soviet Union', in R. H. Marshall, Jr (ed.), *Aspects of Religion in the Soviet Union 1917–1967* (Chicago: University of Chicago Press, 1971), 193–222.

28. Emilio Gentile, *Politics as Religion* (Princeton, NJ: Princeton University Press, 2006), 30.

29. Herbert Butterfield, *Christianity and History* (London: Bell, 1949), 131.

30. The report is published at http://www.glasgowchurchesaction. org.

31. E.g. Dennett, *Breaking the Spell: Religion as a Natural Phenomenon* (London: Penguin, 2007), 287, remarks *en passant* that much of the heavy lifting in America is done by faith-based groups.

32. Cited by Keith Ward, *Is Religion Dangerous?*, 156–7.

33. In what follows I am indebted to the excellent cameo discussion of these issues in John Cornwell, *Darwin's Angel* (London: Profile, 2007), 99ff.

34. John Stuart Mill, 'Autobiography', in *Collected Works*, vol. 1 (Toronto: Toronto University Press, 1981), 35.

35. Jonathan Sacks, 'Why did God Create Atheists', *The Times*, 21 October 2006.

36. This is argued by David F. Ford, 'Faith and Universities in a Secular World', in *Shaping Theology: Engagements in a Religious and Secular World* (Oxford: Blackwell, 2007), 115–42.

37. Bernard Crick, *Guardian*, 22 October, 2005. See http://www. guardian.co.uk/politics/2005/oct/22/religion.world

6

SACRED TEXTS: HOW SHOULD WE READ THEM?

A text may be regarded as sacred by virtue of its origin or function in the community of faith. In most accounts of Scriptural authority, both elements—origin and function—are invoked to describe the canonical status that the text occupies for believers. Its production is the result of some special process of divine inspiration or guidance in relation to the text's human authors and editors. At the same time, it exercises a function of directing belief and practice within the community that acknowledges its religious status. In doing so, the text continues to communicate the presence and speech of God for contemporary hearers. The consequence of this is that there is a continual return to the ancient words, a need to study and recite these in worship, prescribed rules for faithful reading, an awareness of traditional patterns of interpretation, and arguments about their meaning in the present. Even within western Christianity there are significant disputes as to how exactly all of these practices are to be followed. These differences are magnified in relation to the rather different account that Muslims offer of the divine status of the Qur'an. However, similar commitments to reading, hearing, and interpreting are all apparent, alongside a trust in the capacity of the text to communicate the being and will of God.

Critics of religion sometimes claim that this is irrational and dangerous. They insist that there is no warrant for believing that there was some privileged communication of God to ancient persons that will never be superseded by subsequent revelations. The plurality of such claims, moreover, implies that at most only one can be true. A simpler and better assumption is that they are all mistaken. A scrutiny of the texts reveals them to be embedded in the cultural circumstances and assumptions of historical periods very different from our own. To lift these out of context and then transplant them into our own is manifestly absurd. In practice, we have a selective process that reflects not so much the past but our context-dependent prejudices that we project onto that past. We might think that our standards and practices reflect a timeless revelation delivered once for all, but the reality is more complex. Often we select, discriminate, and interpret in ways that are somewhat different from our ancestors.

Much of the attack on sacred texts actually commits the same kind of error that is elsewhere condemned in fundamentalist traditions. The verses are simply fork-lifted out of their original historical setting. They are then treated without reference to standard methods for reading, and it is assumed that they are or ought consistently to be applied as a guide to faith, morals, and politics, independently of communal patterns of interpretation. After surveying a series of the most terrible texts in the Hebrew Bible, Dawkins then concludes, 'What makes my jaw drop is that people today should base their lives on such an appalling role model as Yahweh—and, even worse, that they should bossily try to force the same evil monster (whether fact or fiction) on the rest of us.'[1] Yet no work of criticism or tradition of interpretation is engaged by Dawkins in this reading of the text. All we are told is that a symbolic reading of difficult passages is a 'favourite trick'[2] of religious leaders. The parallels with a crude type of Protestantism are significant. Today's secular critics assume that Scripture is read privately and immediately by its modern readers without recourse to traditions, skills, and established practices of reading. Here again attention fails to be given to the practical and shared aspects of faith. In what follows, I shall argue that a more 'Catholic' account of Scriptural reading is required if we are to make sense of what happens not just in Christianity but in Judaism and Islam also.

Elsewhere, however, Dawkins himself proves capable of more constructive criticism of Scripture in his extolling of the literary merits of the Authorised Version and of the numerous moral aphorisms that it affords. He even remarks in a throw-away sentence that 'we can retain a sentimental loyalty to the cultural and literary traditions of, say, Judaism, Anglicanism or Islam, and even participate in religious rituals such as marriages and funerals, without buying into the supernatural beliefs that historically went along with those traditions'.[3] His remarks here are of some significance for this is precisely what happens in the practice of faith. People participate in rites of passages and appropriate cultural traditions but without a wholesale commitment to a set of beliefs exactly identical with those that commanded the loyalty of their ancestors. To dismiss this as incidental and irrelevant is to miss the point. The reading of sacred texts takes place within communities of faith with their traditions and practices of interpretation. The text is not merely read but is used in prayer, sacraments, credal statements, liturgy, and ritual. Some sections are prioritized over others. Key ethical precepts are excerpted and used for instruction.

One wonders whether the formal hostility to Scripture in Dawkins and Harris is to be explained in part by the very different role occupied by historical texts in the natural sciences. For each generation of scientist there is not the constant return to canonical writings and their contested interpretations, as one finds by contrast in the humanities. The student of political philosophy may usefully engage with Aristotle's *Politics* and in doing so make a significant contribution to that discipline. We never reach a stage of enquiry when the classical works become redundant or of historical interest only. These may be complemented by fresh writing and interpretation, but always the progression in the present will be through a return to canonical texts. It would be wrong to depict the natural sciences as having no need or interest in returning to the writings of its most significant figures. Nevertheless, most of what a young research scientist will read about his or her discipline will be from recent textbooks that represent consensus findings, and not directly through engagement with the writings of Newton, Darwin, and Einstein. There is no need here to return to primary sources from earlier centuries and still less to grant them a normative or authoritative status.

A further explanatory element in this hostility to ancient texts may be the unspoken assumption that we are better than our ancestors. This seems to inform much of the moral distaste surrounding the Bible and the Qur'an. Dawkins, for example, writes about the moral *Zeitgeist* in a way that seems to assume its superiority. What is offered is a Whiggish narrative of moral change. He writes, 'There are local and temporary setbacks such as the United States is suffering from its government in the early 2000s. But over the longer timescale, the progressive trend is unmistakable and it will continue.'[4] In some ways, this must be correct. We would not advocate religious tolerance today if we did not believe that former generations were wrong in persecuting those regarded as heretics, infidels, and dissenters. Arguments against slavery and in support of votes for women are seldom heard today, simply because they have been won. The debates are now over. Yet other than a nod towards 'temporary setbacks' there is little sense in Dawkins that one age may regress in its moral perception from an earlier one. But are we sufficiently confident that our attitudes towards war, death, animals, and children are in most respects much improved on those held by our forebears in the eighteenth century? When scrutinized, Dawkins' own consequentialist argument for abortion may cause some hesitation. The salient issue for him is over whether an embryo is capable of suffering and not whether it is human. But this takes him onto an obvious slippery slope. If we can treat people in ways that merely ensure that they suffer no pain, can we then do to them anything at all including killing them? Aborting foetuses is okay but killing newborn babies is probably not, he suggests, only because we have to draw a line somewhere. Yet this will strike many readers as a highly controversial and unstable position, and not the kind of consensus view to which he believes all reasonable people will be drawn in the absence of religious distortion.

Norman Kemp Smith, a leading Scottish philosopher of the twentieth century, argued that the tendencies of human nature are such that there is no linear and irreversible path of moral progress or metaphysical understanding discernible in human history. The record is mixed, which is just what one might expect from flawed persons. The task of the humanities is therefore a revisiting of ancient texts to ascertain their wisdom and the ways in which this might be critically appropriated in each generation. The fundamental options in understanding our selves and our world are never resolved; uneasy compromises have to be renegotiated in each generation through the revisiting of earlier problems and positions. Hence the disputes between monists and pluralists, realists and idealists, behaviourists and subjectivists, far from being settled, are waged again and again albeit under different circumstances. The study of philosophy thus requires a close acquaintance with its history. It is a mistake to assume that our philosophical comprehension of the world can proceed along progressivist lines modelled by a natural science.[5]

Another critic of religion, Christopher Hitchens, assumes that if not everything in the Bible happened literally in the way that is narrated, then we can dismiss the entire text as worthless. He even comes close to suggesting that Jesus may never have existed on the grounds that some sections of the gospels contain mythological elements. The multiple authors, he says, 'cannot agree on anything of importance.'[6] Again this is eerily reminiscent of fundamentalist resistance to criticism, which fears a deck-of-cards effect as soon as any portion of the text is challenged as other than literally true. This results in a declared strategy of not embarking on criticism because of its perceived corrosive effects. Such views should not detain us. They would not be taken seriously by any reputable scholar within the guild of biblical criticism, let alone within historical study more broadly. They are as simplistic to biblical criticism as creationist science is to biology.

What tends not to be noticed by these critics is that a process of interpretation and wrestling with texts is already under way in the Bible itself. If one thinks of a literal reading of a text as the one that recovers the historical sense of the words, then we can see that both the Bible itself and church tradition invite interpretations that are more complex than this. The historical sense is roughly what the text would have meant to the writer and the reader at the time when it was first written. This recovery of a plain, historical meaning is of course an important element in any critical strategy and it has been prioritized since the Renaissance. Yet it does not exhaust or determine all legitimate readings of the text. There are tensions, conflicting trends, qualifications, and corrections running through Scripture. These are inherent in the texts and we must assume that the compilers of the canon were fully aware of this. So we have different accounts of the history of Israel in Kings and Chronicles, two discrete creation stories at the opening of Genesis, alternative views on the relationship between sin and suffering, a belief in the resurrection of the dead that adjusts earlier annihilationist views, and so on. The list is extensive.[7] This plurality of voices in the text is not the discovery of a modern, critical age. Editors, scribes, and exegetes were aware of them from the very beginning and wrestled with them in their interpretive readings. Jesus himself must be numbered amongst these interpreters. In the sermon on the mount he shows both a formal loyalty to the words of Moses and yet a readiness to interpret them in ways that stretch and qualify their meaning at almost every turn.[8] So the *lex talionis* of an eye for an eye, which incidentally makes good sense in Darwinian terms, is to be transcended by a principle of loving one's enemies and doing good to those that abuse us.

Non-literal, symbolic readings are not the invention of recent critics influenced by secular trends. These are present already in the ways in which the New Testament writers adapt the prophecies of the Hebrew Scriptures, seeing in them a fulfilment that could not have been evident in the historical context in which they first appeared. This pattern of figural interpretation is followed in the early church. Justin Martyr reads Isaiah's prophecy that the government shall be upon his shoulders to be fulfilled in the nailing of Christ to the cross. In the Alexandrian exegesis of Clement and Origen, we find a commitment to allegorical patterns of interpretation that place the meaning of the text in relation to later theological understandings of its fundamental content. Instead of being confined to an original historical context, the text now speaks to the religious and moral concerns of the contemporary church audience.

Following John Cassian in the early fifth century, later typology posits four layers of meaning that can be superimposed upon one another—the historical, the allegorical, the moral, and the mystical. The standard example offered is of Jerusalem—it signifies variously the city of the Jews, the church of Christ, the human soul, and the eternal kingdom of God. The fourfold division of meaning was expressed in the rhyme set out by Nicholas of Lyra.

> The letter teaches events
> Allegory what you should believe
> Tropology what you should do
> Anagogy where you should aim.[9]

Much debate in the middle ages was around ways of controlling such exegesis. Aquinas, for example, attached a greater priority to the literal sense, although claiming that this too could be multiple and contain parabolic meanings. At the Reformation, priority was strongly accorded to the historical sense although this did not altogether preclude other interpretations when the text seemed to demand these.

One distinct advantage offered by this account of the layered meaning of the Scriptural text was that it could accommodate a critical attitude towards those passages that were adjudged morally unacceptable. Where they departed from the teaching and example of Christ, a meaning other than the literal one had to be sought. Augustine famously set out an interpretive principle of charity. When a text interpreted literally does not promote the love of God and one's neighbour, then we must read it figuratively.[10] Hence, bashing one's enemies is about the internal discipline of the soul against its vices, not the extermination of one's opponents. While a modern reader might prefer merely to relativize it in light of other more central and morally decisive portions of the text, the principle of charity remains a long-established and necessary practice of interpretation within the church.

Alongside this stratified interpretation of Scripture, a commitment to a rule of faith as a guiding standard can be discerned early in Christian history, particularly in the face of the Gnostic heresy which sought to divide the Old and New Testaments and to separate an inferior God of creation from the true God of redemption. To enable a proper reading of

Scripture, a set of rules was adopted, learned, and recited. This resembled something like an early version of the Apostles' Creed, for example in the teaching of Irenaeus around 200 CE. This *regula fidei* (rule of faith) thus became an organizing principle around which Scriptural interpretation could be shaped. It provides a hermeneutical criterion for discriminating the more important parts of the canon from the less important. If the affirmations of the creed are to be trusted then the four gospels must be viewed at the centre of the canon, unlike say Esther or 2 Peter. It is hard to see how any theology can avoid an interpretive decision of this nature. One is ineluctably committed to making a judgement about the vital themes of Scripture for faith and in light of this to seeking the meaning of hard and obscure passages.

The practice of criticism as it has been pursued in seminaries, colleges, and universities for the last two hundred years has settled on some standard critical tools for the interpreting of sacred texts. You might not know this from the recent attack on religion. These methods include a commitment to textual criticism which seeks to establish the most reliable—usually the earliest—versions of the writings now available to us. This is accompanied by the study of these texts in their original languages and with reference to the historical circumstances in which they were spoken, written, transmitted, and edited. All this is the standard fare of traditio-historical criticism and lies behind good translation of the texts. No translation may be devoid of elements of interpretation and none may be uniquely privileged, but there are normative practices employed by the translator and exegete that cannot evade these philological and historical disciplines.[11]

The earlier strategy of reconstructing authorial intention is now discredited for several reasons. As a psychological entity, it is simply not recoverable, not even by the recollection of the author. The notion that the real meaning might lie behind its public expression fails to recognize that human beings are embodied social persons rather than minds that lurk some-where inside our heads. And in any case, the meaning of the text is neither reducible to nor limited by whatever was in the author's mind at the time of writing. Despite this intentional fallacy, however, the historical study of the text does have the task of establishing what it sought to communicate in its orig-inal setting and perhaps also in that of later redactors. Further interpretive meanings can be elicited from the text but these generally need to be broadly consistent with the trajectories of meaning established by the historical critic.

A critical reading of the text is always demanded because Scripture itself seems to offer a standard by which its various parts must be assessed. At least, this appears to be a conse-quence of the chronological sequence in which the church has organized the canon of the Old and New Testaments. This itself represents an implicit rule of faith already at work. Each hermeneutical act implies a judgement about what the central subject matter (what German scholars have called the *Sache*) of the sacred texts comprises. In light of this, the different com-ponent parts are organized and interpreted critically. Some may even be rejected as mere cultural accretions that conceal the subject matter or represent a declension from it. In the history of the church, Martin Luther provides the clearest example of this strategy. While accepting the medieval account of inspiration, he seems at the same time to develop another approach based upon an understanding of its function and content within the life of the church. The primary function of the Bible under the providence of God is to bear witness to the gospel of Christ and in light of this we are to read and teach its parts. This creates something like the concept of a canon within the canon, thus enabling Luther to prioritize John's Gospel, Romans, and 1 Peter. It also generated a famously negative attitude to the epistle of James, a 'right strawy' epistle which he regarded as obscuring the gospel of free grace. He could even remark cheerfully that one of those days he would light the fire with Jimmy.[12] Nevertheless, Luther accepted that James must remain within the canon, to be studied and assessed by later generations of interpreters. Many of them, including Calvin, sought to reconcile it with Luther's theology of the gospel.

The interpretation of Scripture is never fixed or settled at any period in the history of the church. The constant transmission and translation of its content requires fresh interpretation. Disputes about slavery, the role of women, the Sabbath, democracy, divorce, homosexuality, and war have in part been about contested interpretations of sacred texts. These have often reflected an argument about whether the central subject matter of Scripture can trump particular texts that point towards a different set of conclusions. For example, does the equality of persons in the sight of God and the abrogation of social distinction in the church require the rejection of slavery as an institution, despite many passages that appear to acknowledge and tacitly accept it? This question was answered in the affirmative by abolitionists against opponents who appealed to the letter of the text.

There is a captivating discussion of this in Mark Noll's recent study *The Civil War as a Theological Crisis*.[13] He notes that the dispute between advocates of slavery and abolitionists was to a large extent about the correct interpretation of Scripture. To those on one side, the plain sense of Scripture was clear with many passages condoning the institution of slavery and no sign of any prohibition by Jesus. On the other side, another body of opinion emerged. This regarded slavery as inconsistent with the most central ethical injunctions of Scripture to love one's neighbour, to seek justice, to show mercy, and to love one another in the body of Christ. To many this seemed a dangerous strategy since it relegated to a historical context those passages of the text that offered support for slavery. In the end, Noll notes sadly that the correct interpretation of Scripture was delegated to the army generals. At the same time, from a European perspective, the dispute revealed the hopelessness of allowing individuals and small groups freedom to read the text without the controlling hand of a national church body or the Roman magisterium. What makes Noll's study so intriguing is our retrospective and uncontested conviction that the abolitionists were fundamentally right. Their preference for the spirit rather than the letter prevailed and is now universally acknowledged. It seems that this particular debate about the right interpretation of Scripture is now over. Furthermore, what we can also see is that abolitionist interpreters benefited from the influence of secular thought. Theories of human rights, the dignity and autonomy of each person, a conviction about the value of the individual—all these were powerful Enlightenment themes that came to shape positively the reading of Scripture.

As we have already noted, the process of interpretation or 'critical traditioning' is already underway in Scripture itself. The text contains comment, correction, revision, and adjustment of its own meanings. The process of redaction is itself part of the tradition, thus creating a tension between what is given and held by the community and the ways in which it must constantly wrestle with its meaning. Christian theology has come to a clearer recognition of this in dialogue with Jewish rabbinic traditions. These include not only a commitment to preserving and transmitting a deposit of authoritative texts but also an ongoing wrestling with its meaning under new circumstances, a process already evident within a canon that contains multiple and sometimes conflicting meanings. Ellen Davis explores this in relation to the treatment of the Canaanites in the Hebrew Scriptures.[14] The official Deuteronomic party line is that they are God's enemies and deserve to be slaughtered. This is a view that is impossibly difficult to sustain, especially for Palestinian Christians, and one winces at the attempts of earlier western commentators to justify it.[15] The apparently liberating narrative of the exodus is conjoined to a more problematic account of conquest, a fact that has often been overlooked by western exegetes. On the other hand, as Davis notes, there are different voices in the text that need to be sifted to establish a better trajectory of interpretation. Those Canaanites who are named after the conquest, for example Rahab, are generally commended for displaying a courage and faithfulness more commendable than that of the Israelites. And in Matthew's Gospel, the acknowledgement of the Canaanite woman by Jesus matches the parabolic example of the Good Samaritan in extending the commandment to love one's neighbour to foreigners and out-groups. The Bible itself reflects this tension and provides traditions of interpretation that challenge and revise other tendencies of the text. So Davis writes, 'A tradition earns its authority through long rumination on the past. A living tradition is a potentially courageous form of shared consciousness, because a tradition, in contrast to an ideology, preserves (in some form) our mistakes and atrocities, as well as our insights and moral victories.'[16]

In discussing these issues, Hendrikus Berkhof, a Dutch Reformed theologian, identifies four layers of meaning that the interpreter must recognize in Scripture.[17] What is interesting about this stratification is that almost every example he cites is contested. These levels of interpretive significance comprise: (i) the direct witness to the events of divine self-disclosure, for example the exodus, the revelation of the prophets, the praise of the Psalms, and the story of Jesus; (ii) the insights that immediately arise from this witness, e.g. the confession of the creation of the world, the themes of sin and grace, and the hope of eternal life; (iii) those figurative or symbolic expressions that also represent these themes although less directly, e.g. stories of angels and the devil, and narratives of the end times; and (iv) other representations that are more culturally limited and can be quickly relativized, e.g. patriarchal assumptions about women, belief in demon possession, the three-storey universe, the sacrificial cult, and dietary laws. Berkhof points out that almost every text contains some combination of these levels of meaning. References to the sacrificial cult in the New Testament are generally directed towards the story of Jesus. Conversely, the exodus narratives and the gospel stories may be overlaid with elements of myth or social assumptions that we no longer share.

One might shift the pieces around and locate the various elements of Scripture at different levels of meaning. Yet this itself confirms the necessity of an interpretive strategy that distinguishes what the text meant in its former settings from what it should mean for the faith community here and now. The task of course is never complete, but always provisional, all conclusions being defeasible and subject to later revision. The most striking illustration from church history of the unavoidable necessity of human interpretive judgements of sacred texts must be the fragmented nature of the Protestant churches. Their commitment to the principle of *sola Scriptura* has not yielded consensus or unanimity under the guidance of the Spirit but a frequent pattern of splintering, seceding, and subsequent reuniting. Much of this attests the shifting understandings of Scripture that prevail across time and space.

Protestantism, with its polemics against papal infallibility and the declensions of some parts of the church from the gospel, has often failed to recognize the significance of tradition. Yet tradition is necessary not simply for the preservation of sacred texts and historic patterns of interpretation, but also for the ongoing, living process of appropriation. The transmission and translation of the faith in new cultural settings bring fresh and challenging readings of Scripture. These, moreover, should not be done by maverick groups and individuals in isolation from the wider church and the resources it offers. The principle of *sola Scriptura* can easily lapse into arbitrary and irresponsible readings of texts when outside the discipline of established practices and habits of textual interpretation.

For this reason too, the work of theological education is a necessary accompaniment to the proclamation and transmission of faith.

> To gain entrance and to find its central perspective the reader (of the Bible) needs help. The community of believers must offer an introduction, a guide, a summary. This is a daring undertaking which nevertheless, in reliance on the guidance of the Spirit, must be undertaken, and which through the centuries has been undertaken.[18]

Tradition need not be presented as if it were a pure, smoothly flowing stream. It may have its stagnant pools, its tributaries leading nowhere, and its broken banks. Yet it remains a necessary corollary of the church's sacred texts with their chronological shape, gospel centre, and convictions about the ongoing action of the Spirit. Tradition can function through preaching, instruction, creeds, catechisms, books, the lives of the saints, study groups, magazines, and websites. To read Scripture without reference to the varied and living testimony of the community across time and space is to displace it from its proper location.

Is there ever a time when a reading of Scripture must be anathematized, its exponents excommunicated? Does the church ever find itself in a *status confessionis*, when a divergent reading of Scripture must be condemned as outside the legitimate bounds of disagreement and subsequent conversation? This is widely believed to have happened at least twice in the last century in the experience of the confessing church in Nazi Germany and in the rejection of apartheid as a heresy by the ecumenical church. The imposition of anti-Jewish legislation by the Hitler regime in 1933 was regarded as creating a *status confessionis* by Bonhoeffer and others. In South Africa, the theological defence of apartheid by Dutch Calvinists was similarly regarded as so transgressing the meaning of Scripture that it called into question the proper identity of the church. More recently, Naim Ateek suggests that a *status confessionis* has arisen around Palestinian suicide bombings and Israeli attacks on civilian populations.[19] There seem to be limits therefore on the plurality of interpretations that can be permitted, yet the gravity of these examples may suggest that such limiting situations are quite rare. For example, if Christian groups were to advocate suicide bombings on civilian targets then we might expect a similar reaction of denunciation and formal anathematizing. Yet the normal process of conversation, study, dialogue, and an awaiting of outcomes seems better suited to managing most interpretive disagreements.

The standard Christian theological appropriation of the Bible draws attention to its narrative structure, its focus on the four gospels, and the human coefficient of the authors that demands critical, historical study. It is sometimes assumed that if other faiths were to adopt similar strategies with respect to their sacred texts then a greater degree of consensus could be achieved. In what follows, however, I shall argue that this is neither necessary nor sufficient for better understanding, but that nevertheless there exists in other faiths a similarly important role for fluid interpretive traditions.

Jewish scholars complain that theological readings of the Hebrew Bible typically reflect Christian tendencies. The need for the organization of disparate materials may itself reflect something of the western desire to systematize that is felt more acutely by Christian than Jewish thinkers. The integration of philosophy with theology that has characterized Christian theology from the early centuries is not attempted, with some notable exceptions, in the less speculative traditions of Judaism and Islam. Within Judaism, the impulse to systematize finds expression instead in the law, with its commentaries on how the Torah is to be interpreted and lived in the community of faith. Here we find less anxiety to find a single idea that acts as an organizing principle for the interpretation of the entire canon. Jewish interpretation is not dominated by the search for a centre to the Bible, whether election, covenant, or the mighty acts of God—each of which has been proposed by successive Old Testament theologians. According to Jon Levenson, 'Jewish biblical theology is likely to be, as it always has been, a matter of piecemeal observations appended to the text and subordinate to its particularity.'[20]

The emergence of rabbinic interpretation after the destruction of Jerusalem in 70 CE reveals something significant about the interplay between a fixed canon and communal strategies of interpretation. The Hebrew Bible itself contains an interplay of interpretive forces, but once the canon was closed—no further additions to Scripture being permitted—then types of interpretation emerged that constantly return to the texts but in ways that are selective and imaginative. The act of interpretation presupposes the sacredness of the text but it also has the task of revealing its meaning for the present—it must reactualize it as the divine Word. Michael Fishbane speaks about the singularity of Scripture residing in 'the depth of possibilities for true teaching, the legal and theological experience, latent in the text'. He quotes the words of one midrashic commentary: 'When the Holy One, blessed be He, gave the Torah to Israel, He only gave it as wheat from which to extract flour, and as flax wherewith to weave a garment.'[21] It is as if the critical and creative discernment of the interpreter is a corollary of their being a sacred text at all. This work, moreover, takes places within a community of practice. So key passages of the Hebrew Scriptures are used as lectionaries for Sabbaths, as recitations for festivals and fasts, as the focus of public expositions and sermons, and in the reading and praying of the Psalms.[22] These activities all regulate the use and function of Scripture in the synagogue.

A good example of creative interpretation is found in the dispute between the Houses of Shammai and Hillel on the correct physical position for reciting the Shema.[23] According to Deuteronomy 6:7, it is to be recited 'when you lie down and when you rise up'. One school of thought, the Shammaites, proposed that one must actually recline in the evening and stand up in the morning while reciting. Against this, the Hillelites argued that these expressions simply referred to whatever one was ordinarily doing at that time of day. So there was no requirement to be literally lying down or standing up when saying the Shema. Moreover, despite their literalism, even the Shammaites had to employ some critical discernment in establishing when and how often the Shema was to be recited and exactly which words were to be employed.

In approaching the Qur'an, we encounter obvious differences not experienced in dialogue between Jewish and Christian theologians. Unlike the Hebrew Bible and even the New Testament, the text was produced in a relatively short timespan, perhaps just over twenty years. Written in one language and generated from a single source, it achieved canonical status almost immediately. Unlike the Tanakh or the Bible, it has a self-referential quality. The writings display a reflexive awareness of their identity as sacred scripture, to the extent of recognizing their own uniqueness and unsurpassability.

The revelations to Muhammad cover different phases of his life so that the surahs of the Qur'an can be divided into Meccan and Medinan periods. Unable himself to write, Muhammad was dependent for the subsequent transmission of his revelations on an oral tradition of recitation and scribes who wrote down his words. After his death, the immediate history of the text is unclear although it is widely assumed that in the time of the third caliph, Uthman, a concerted attempt was made less than twenty years after the prophet's death to prepare an authoritative version of the text.[24] This involved examination of all written collections and the interviewing of persons who had memorized portions of the text. This 'Uthmanic' text became the basis of the Qur'an as we have it today. Some western depictions of the text as unstable and evolving over two centuries resemble work that has been undertaken by Protestant biblical scholars, most notably that of Wansbrough.[25]

However, it seems that such a radical revision of the traditional understanding of Qur'anic origins has not commanded widespread scholarly support. Notwithstanding issues around variant readings of the text and differences in style, content, and context within the Qur'an, it is generally recognized that we are dealing with a sacred book that was produced more rapidly and exhibits a much greater degree of historical focus and self-consciousness than the sacred texts of the other Abrahamic faiths. More plausible perhaps is the historical approach of Angelika Neuwirth who sees in the Qur'an, or at least its Meccan surahs, the representation of earlier liturgical forms used for regular recitation. These reflect a single, historical origin in the life of the prophet rather than a centuries-long process of redaction by multiple editors in a variety of contexts.[26]

Further differences involve the lack of a chronological structure in the Qur'an, its 114 surahs being organized largely in relation to their length, beginning with the longest, rather than on a single timeline or thematic shaping. This often frustrates western readers who expect a narrative structure similar to that of Genesis or the four gospels. Intended for recitation as well as reading, the Arabic text has a divine quality for Muslims that is generally not matched by Jewish and Christian Scriptures. The stress on Bible translation, moreover, is a feature of Christian mission that is not reflected in Islam with its greater devotion to the Arabic. One cannot even talk about the original text insofar as there is only one text, all translations lacking authoritative status. The revelatory quality is thus largely lost in translation. The true worship of God requires commitment to public Arabic recitation. Unlike a family Bible, the Qur'an is not a book which is read silently in personal acts of devotion. It is recited aloud in public. The word *qur'an* comes from *qara'a* meaning 'to read aloud or to recite'. This covers the initial act of presenting the revealed text to Muhammad, his subsequent repetition of the words to his companions, the text of the

Qur'an as it was constituted, and finally the public recitation
of its words.[27]

   This last point reflects a further possible difference from
Judaism and Christianity. The revelation of God is not so
much *from* Muhammad, or even *through* him, but strictly
speaking *to* him. The prophet does not speak himself or offer
comment on what is revealed; his task is to read what is 'sent
down', an expression that occurs over 200 times. As the messenger, not the author of the text, Muhammad receives an
extended series of revelations that are recited and subsequently
recorded in the Qur'an. The other sacred writings of the people of the book are themselves acknowledged as authoritative
but these are surpassed by the Qur'an which has a qualitatively
different status for Muslims. Some parallels can be found for
this account of inspiration in Jewish views of the Torah, in
medieval theories of dictation, and in the Protestant account
of plenary inspiration. Nevertheless, this high view of the text
seems to be a distinguishing feature of Islam both by virtue
of the Qur'an's self-understanding and also of the subsequent
role that it plays in the life of the community. For this reason, it has been suggested by exponents of Christian–Muslim
dialogue that the appropriate parallel is not so much between
the Qur'an and the Bible but between the Qur'an and Jesus.[28]
For Christians, it is Jesus whose being has an irreducible divine
status, whereas for Muslims the Qur'an is of all created realities
the most revealing of Allah's will and nature. The parallel is
imperfect since Jesus is worshipped in a way in which the
Qur'an is not, but in terms of finality, unsurpassability, and
salvific power there are some significant similarities.

We sent down the Qur'an with the truth, and with the truth it has
come down—[Prophet], We sent you only to give good news and
warning—it is a recitation that We have revealed in parts, so that
you can recite it to people at intervals; We have sent it down little
by little. Say, 'Whether you believe it or not, those who were given
knowledge earlier fall down on their faces when it is recited to them,

and say, "Glory to our Lord! Our Lord's promise has been fulfilled." They fall down on their faces, weeping and [the Qur'an] increases their humility.'[29]

Some western commentators have argued for greater recognition of the human coefficient in the process of transmission. Islam needs to move in this direction, they claim. This would allow for a relativizing of some texts, in acknowledgement that they are conditioned by the historical setting in which they emerged, thus mitigating against the dangers of a simple literal reading of passages taken out of context. This is the strategy favoured by Hans Küng. Stressing the need for historical study of the reception, setting, and transmission of the text, he goes on to argue that Islamic scholarship is now undergoing the travails that beset Jewish and Christian critics last century.

In 1971, in Kabul, at that time still the peaceful capital of Afghanistan, I reached agreement with a Muslim professor in a long evening of discussion among friends that the Qur'anic word of God is at the same time the human word of the Prophet. I asked my conversation partner whether he could put forward such a view at the university. His reply was a clear no: 'If I did, I would have to emigrate.' And indeed, he did, some years later.[30]

Küng can claim some support for his approach in recent Muslim scholarship, particularly in the west. In a recent volume, Muhammed Kalisch, a professor in Münster, argues boldly that the Qur'an is the record of the spiritual experience of Muhammad.[31] Like other holy books, it can be described symbolically as a revelation from God. Yet it needs to be read in context and not as a literal historical record. This strategy tends to position the authority of the Qur'an in ways that parallel the work of Jewish and Christian scholars. It is a courageous move yet perhaps unlikely to command widespread support within his own faith community. It requires a significant revision to the account of Qur'anic origins that we find in the Qur'an itself and held by the vast majority of Muslims. A different approach might distinguish between the authority of the text and the ways in which it demands interpretation. This is the preferred method of the philosopher Aref Nayed in his response to Cardinal Tauran's recent criticism of Islamic views of the Qur'an. He argues that the Qur'an is eternal, original, and essentially divine in its discourse, but he goes on to claim that this has never prevented scholars from recognizing that it unfolds historically as it is revealed to the prophet in the particular circumstances of his life and that of the later community. 'Muslim scholars were always aware of the fact that the activities of interpretation, understanding, and exegesis of God's eternal discourse are forms of human strenuous striving that must be dutifully renewed in every believing generation.'[32] Cardinal Tauran's suggestion that dialogue is impeded by the Muslim belief that the Qur'an is dictated by God thus fails to take into account the extent to which all readings of the text are shaped by long-established schools of interpretation.

Common Word is a recent inter-faith initiative by leading Muslim scholars in the world. It reveals a commitment to discussion of how Islamic interpretive traditions function particularly in relation to patterns of reasoning in Judaism and Christianity.[33] Yet to demand of them an abandonment of traditional convictions surrounding Qur'anic authority seems no more promising a pre-condition for dialogue than asking Christians to forsake the Nicene Creed or the divinity of Christ. The expression 'common word' is itself drawn from the Qur'an, which speaks about the importance of the people of the book finding a statement of faith that can be shared. 'People of the Book, let us arrive at a statement that is common to us all: we worship God alone.'[34]

The frequent citation of traditional readings in *Common Word* illustrates the significance of historical interpretation for a right understanding of the Qur'an. According to the standard account, the exegesis of the Prophet himself in the Hadith already begins this process, followed by that of his companions and his successors.[35] So began a process of transmission and interpretation that divided into different schools of interpretation, most notably Sunni and Shi'a. The precise application of the Qur'an to everyday life is mediated by emerging and contested traditions concerning the sayings and actions of the Prophet. These develop across changing circumstances. Rough parallels are often drawn here with the role of the Talmud in Judaism, and with tradition in Roman Catholicism, although like the former and unlike the latter there is no central magisterium determining legitimate interpretation.[36]

All of this is commonplace. Yet it should be sufficient to refute the simplistic assumption that a sacred text functions literally, ahistorically, and in isolation from recognized schools and methods of interpretation. Some forms of Protestantism with their individualism and naïve credulity may function in this way. And to that extent, recent secular criticism of religion resembles its flip-side. Too little attention is paid to scholarly traditions of study and close textual reasoning, the function of texts in the life of communities, and the way in which interpretation shifts across time by embodying new insights and facing fresh challenge. Islam too has its exegetical traditions that engage constructively with democracy, economic development, and the rights of women.

The sceptic may concede the necessity of critical interpretation and appropriation, but may still claim that the sheer plurality of sacred scriptures must inevitably induce doubts about the claims of each of them. There is no simple rejoinder to this challenge—traditional appeals to miracles no longer hold up as external proofs of those Scriptures that attest them. Our sacred texts cannot be proven as authoritative to outsiders or sceptics by any single argument, any more than can our most deeply held religious beliefs. Here again their worth and rationality are displayed, rather than demonstrated, through the ways they function in the practice of the believing community. Attention requires to be given to the ways in which people live and act, their capacity to love God and neighbour, and the practical uses to which they put their texts. But what is now vitally important is a shift in the way that faith communities themselves regard the sacred texts of other religions.

In recognizing the plurality of sacred texts one does not need to see these as mutually destructive, nor as corrosive of one's own faith in a particular tradition. They have indeed different histories, functions, and patterns of interpretation. But maintaining a commitment to any one should not require the dismissal of all the others. One does not have to establish simple binary oppositions between them to display a loyalty to one's own faith. This may well prove the major religious challenge of the twenty-first century—to find ways of affirming the presence and activity of God in other faiths, without losing a sense of the distinctiveness and value of one's own. During the twentieth century, the ecumenical movement within the churches ended centuries of suspicion in a series of dialogues that yielded greater recognition of different traditions—both in terms of what was held in common and what was distinctive. Since the Holocaust, Christians have finally engaged in closer dialogue with Jews and have come to repent of the anti-Semitism that has scarred the history of the church. In doing so, different and less harmful readings of Scripture have been achieved. Today the task must be extended to other faiths, particularly Islam. Since more than half of the world's population confesses Christianity or Islam, this task has a political urgency. The informed discussion of the sacred texts of faiths other than one's own is a necessary part of this process.

As a Christian theologian, I am committed to the uniquely transforming power of Jesus, but this should not prevent me from acknowledging the religious value of the Tanakh for Jews and the Qur'an for Muslims. This mutual recognition presents formidable theological challenges but one should not seek premature closure on these questions before a proper engagement with the texts of the other. These must be seen as revelation also for large numbers of men, women, and children. And in the providence of God one can learn more about one's own faith through the encounter with others. At the same time, one needs also to recognize the intellectual integrity and moral commitment of those who profess no faith. We exclude secular critics from the conversation at our peril, for these too have an important role to play in the constantly evolving perceptions of faith communities.

The task of interpreting sacred texts is therefore an unsettled, evolving, and unavoidable responsibility of the faith community. The process of critical reading is already under way in Scripture itself, including the teaching of Jesus and Paul. By contrast, the attempt to read literally and timelessly from the surface of the text, whether by zealots or sceptics, is a modernist aberration that lacks any historical sense or proven communal context.

Notes

1. Dawkins, *The God Delusion*, 248.
2. Ibid., 247.
3. Ibid., 344.
4. Ibid., 271.
5. See *The Credibility of Divine Existence: The Collected Papers of Norman Kemp Smith*, ed. A. J. D. Porteous, R. D. Maclennan, and G. E. Davie (London: Macmillan, 1967). See especially George Davie, 'The Significance of the Philosophical Papers', 63–4.
6. Christopher Hitchens, *God Is Not Great: The Case against Religion* (London: Atlantic Books, 2007), 111.
7. Robert P. Carroll explores many of these tensions within Scripture in *Wolf within the Sheepfold: The Bible as a Problem for Christianity* (London: SPCK, 1991).

8. See Robert Grant, *A Short History of the Interpretation of the Bible* (London: SCM, 1984), 8ff.

9. See C. Ocker, 'Biblical Interpretation in the Middle Ages', in Donald McKim (ed.), *Dictionary of Major Biblical Interpreters* (Downers' Grove, IL: IVP, 2007), 14–21 at 18.

10. Augustine, *On Christian Doctrine*, 3.10.14.

11. This is argued, for example, by James D. G. Dunn, 'Criteria for a Wise Reading of a Biblical Text', in David F. Ford and Graham Stanton (eds.), *Reading Texts, Seeking Wisdom* (London: SCM, 2003), 38–52.

12. Quoted by Brian Gerrish, *The Old Protestantism and the New* (Edinburgh: T& T Clark, 1982), 55.

13. Mark Noll, *The Civil War as a Theological Crisis* (Durham, NC: University of North Carolina Press, 2006).

14. Ellen F. Davis, 'Critical Traditioning: Seeking an Inner Biblical Hermeneutic', in Ellen F. Davis and Richard B. Hays (eds.), *The Art of Reading Scripture* (Grand Rapids, MI: Eerdmans, 2003), 163–80.

15. See the discussion in John Collins, *The Bible After Babel: Historical Criticism in a Postmodern Age* (Grand Rapids, MI: Eerdmans, 2005). 'One of the most troubling aspects of this biblical story is the way it has been used, analogically, over the centuries as a legitimating paradigm of violent conquest—by the Puritans in Ireland and in New England, by the Boers in South Africa, and by right-wing Zionists and their conservative Christian supporters in modern Israel.' (62–3).

16. Ellen F. Davis, 'Critical Traditioning', 168–9.

17. Hendrikus Berkhof, *Christian Faith: An Introduction to the Study of the Faith* (Grand Rapids, MI: Eerdmans, 1979), 97ff.

18. Ibid., 101.

19. Naim Ateek, 'Suicide Bombers: What is Theologically and Morally Wrong with Suicide Bombings? A Palestinian Christian Perspective', *Studies in World Christianity*, 8 (2002), 5–30.

20. Jon D. Levenson, *The Hebrew Bible, the Old Testament, and Historical Criticism* (Philadelphia: Westminster/John Knox Press, 1993), 54.

21. Michael Fishbane, *The Garments of Torah* (Bloomington: Indiana University Press, 1989), 37–8.

22. See Stefan C. Reif, 'Aspects of the Jewish Contribution to Biblical Interpretation', in John Barton (ed.), *Cambridge Companion to*

Biblical Interpretation (Cambridge: Cambridge University Press, 1998), 143–59 at 150.

23. Here I am following the discussion of David Kraemer, 'Scriptural Interpretation in the Mishnah', in Magne Saebø (ed.), *Hebrew Bible/Old Testament: The History of Its Interpretation*, vol. 1 (Göttingen: Vandenhoeck & Ruprecht, 1996), 281.

24. See Fred M. Donner, 'The Historical Context', in Jane Dammen McAuliffe (ed.), *The Cambridge Companion to the Qur'an* (Cambridge: Cambridge University Press, 2006), 23–39.

25. John Wansbrough, *Quranic Studies: Sources and Methods of Scriptural Interpretation* (Oxford: Oxford University Press, 1977).

26. Angelika Neuwirth, 'Qur'an and History—A Disputed Relationship: Some Reflections of Qur'anic History and History in the Qur'an', *Journal of Qur'anic Studies* 5 (2003), 1–18.

27. Hans Küng notes this comparison with the Bible to illustrate the distinctive character of the Qur'an for Muslims. See *Islam: Past, Present and Future* (Oxford: One World, 2007), 63.

28. See for example David Burrell, 'Islam and Christianity', in Ian McFarland et al. (eds.), *Cambridge Dictionary of Theology* (Cambridge: Cambridge University Press, forthcoming).

29. *Qur'an*, trans. M. A. S. Abdel Haleem (Oxford: Oxford University Press, 2004), 17: 105–9.

30. *Islam: Past, Present & Future*, op. cit., 528.

31. Muhammed Kalisch, 'A Muslim View of Judaism', in Perry Schmidt-Leukel and Lloyd Ridgeon (eds.), *Islam and Inter-Faith Relations* (London: SCM, 2007), 67–83.

32. Aref Ali Nayed, 'Interview with Catholic News Service', Islamica Magazine, http://www.islamicamagazine.com/Common-Word/CNS-interview.html

33. See for example the symposium on Scriptural reasoning in *Modern Theology*, 22.3 (2006), 339ff. and David Ford, *Shaping Theology; Engagements in a Religious and Secular World* (Oxford: Blackwell, 2008), 73–90.

34. *Qur'an* 3:64.

35. See Claude Gilliot, 'Exegesis of the Qur'ān: Classical and Medieval', *Encyclopaedia of the Qur'ān*. General Editor: Jane Dammen McAuliffe (Leiden: Brill, 2009), Brill Online. www.brillonline.nl/subscriber/entry?entry=q3_COM-00058 (accessed 11 February 2009).

36. See Küng, *Islam: Past, Present and Future*, 269.

CONCLUSION

WHERE THE HEART PONTIFICATES

DONALD MacKinnon once wrote of the ways in which the differences between faith and unbelief run too deep to be quickly resolved by any intellectual gambit.[1] There is no quick-fix, readily available argument that will bring a final resolution of the questions posed by religion and its critics. And we should beware, therefore, of attempts too readily to defeat our opponents. The preceding discussion has sought to offer a response to recent secular criticism of religion but not in an attempt to win all the spoils. Under the impact of criticism—both internal and external—the self-understanding of religion will change, as a result of textual, moral, historical, philosophical, and theological pressures. To this extent, faith itself is an evolving phenomenon albeit one that is shaped by convictions about the significance of past episodes of history.

The preceding chapters inevitably range across a wide terrain. These have encroached on the disciplines of history, philosophy, theology, psychology, and sociology as well as the natural sciences. This multi-disciplinary path is full of pitfalls—doubtless, I have stumbled into a few—but the excursion at least reveals the extensiveness of those considerations that must be brought to bear in any assessment of religion. In itself, this must show why no one single consideration or argument or insight can settle the issues or defeat one's opponents. Faith or its rejection inevitably engages the will, the intellect, the emotions, and one's total human experience.

> Where the heart pontificates
> There the questions proliferate.[2]

Those lines of R. S. Thomas illustrate the extent to which the largest issues of mind and heart inevitably generate the greatest conundrums. These are not resolvable by glib humanistic platitudes any more than by a fundamentalist commitment to a sacred text or set of credal propositions.

Recent debate has been too adversarial, the shrill denunciations of religion provoking a backlash of vituperative rhetoric and over-extended apologetics. In part, this may be explained by the attraction of stage-managed debates between those holding starkly opposed positions. These generate intense interest in blogs and video clips, with spectators arguing tediously afterwards about winners and losers. Even London buses now advertise the humanist slogan, 'There is probably no God.' Entertaining as these gladiatorial contests may be, they do little to promote goodwill, mutual respect, and the understanding of difference. Intellectual discernment requires, not the approach of the propagandist, but those who are ready carefully to weigh differing opinions, insights, and considerations. What is needed is a more patient conversation, more informed debate, and a readiness to interpret different positions *in optimam partem*. Many humanists, agnostics, and sceptics already participate in this venture—their works deserve a higher profile.

Religion is not about to wither on the vine of secular society. On the contrary, recent evidence suggests that it is globally resurgent if somewhat marginalized amongst western intellectual elites, though even here some shifts are apparent. In any case, as we have seen, if some of the conclusions advanced by cognitive psychologists about our disposition to think and behave religiously are even close to the mark then we can predict the persistence of religion in human societies. The challenge, then, is not one of eradication but of better understanding in the hope that religion can function as a source of well-being for its practitioners. In speaking of the 'broken middle', Gillian Rose argued for an inhabiting of the difficult spaces between fixed positions and ancient certainties in which so often the truth is to be discerned. This negotiation can be uncomfortable, challenging, and hard work. But we need to attempt it, whether as believers or unbelievers, not in the expectation that an easy consensus will emerge but in the hope that we will be chastened and illumined in our different ways by that undertaking. Too much of the debate assumes that the issues can be foreclosed once for all, as if sudden progress on the most fundamental questions about the nature of the world, the self, and God can now be achieved. This optimism, I suggest, is misplaced. The record of history is that these disputes will continue to be debated and negotiated as long as there are human beings to undertake the task. What this also underlines, moreover, is the extent to which something like a faith commitment is involved in whatever worldview and self-understanding we adopt, together with the moral and spiritual dispositions we develop. Far from being an egregious act of unreason in the face of contrary evidence, a commitment seems an unavoidable feature of our human condition.

What has been offered is a defence of faith against criticism. But it is not one that seeks to evade its difficulties, its mixed historical record, or the implausible forms that it sometimes takes. There is something to be learned from critics, even deeply hostile ones. The power to see ourselves as others see us enables a healthy form of criticism in religion, as in much else. We can be rescued from hyper-beliefs that are implausible; upon inspection, these might turn out to be less vital to our faith than once we imagined. Jesus himself was a fierce critic of some forms of religious belief and organization—his crucifixion was a consequence of the collusion of the combined forces of law and religion.

The response to criticism need not be a wholly negative exercise in defensive apologetics. It can yield fresh insight and new ways of approaching one's subject. The foregoing does not attempt a full defence of a particular faith position—it has been a more preliminary exercise of exploring sympathetically the wider terrain in which religion is positioned. Despite centuries of scepticism and critical attack, the curious persistence of faith even amongst philosophers, scientist, and artists, suggests its capacity to order life by a standard not of our own making and to impart a wisdom from earlier ages that can still be ours today.

Notes

1. 'The issues between faith and unbelief go too deep, and cut too sharply, for revival of metaphysical idealist gambits effectively to resolve them.' Donald MacKinnon, *Borderlands in Theology* (London: Lutterworth, 1968), 89.
2. R. S. Thomas, 'Play', in *Collected Later Poems 1998–2000* (Tarset: Bloodaxe Books, 2004), 290.

BIBLIOGRAPHY

AHMED, AKBAR S. *Living Islam: From Samarkand to Stornoway* (London: BBC, 1993).

APPLEBY, R. SCOTT. *The Ambivalence of the Sacred: Religion, Violence and Reconciliation* (New York: Rowman & Littlefield, 2000).

ATEEK, NAIM. 'Suicide Bombers: What is Theologically and Morally Wrong with Suicide Bombings? A Palestinian Christian Perspective', *Studies in World Christianity*, 8 (2002), 5–30.

ATRAN, SCOTT. *In Gods We Trust: The Evolutionary Landscape of Religion* (New York: Oxford University Press, 2002).

AUGUSTINE. *On Christian Doctrine* (Edinburgh: T&T Clark, 1873).

AUSTIN, GREG, TODD KRANOCK, and THOM OOMMEN. 'God and War: An Audit & Explanation', http://news.bbc.co.uk/1/shared/spl/hi/world/04/war_audit_pdf/pdf/war_audit.pdf

BARLOW, HUGH. *Dead for Good: Martyrdom and the Rise of the Suicide Bomber* (London: Paradigm, 2007).

BARRETT, JUSTIN L. *Why Would Anyone Believe in God?* (Lanham, MD: Altamira Press, 2004).

BEATTIE, TINA. *The New Atheists: The Twilight of Reason and the War on Religion* (London: Darton, Longman & Todd, 2007).

BEHE, MICHAEL. *Darwin's Black Box* (New York: Free Press, 1996).

BEIT-HALLAHIM, BENJAMIN. 'Atheist: A Psychological Profile', in Michael Martin (ed.), *Cambridge Companion to Atheism* (Cambridge: Cambridge University Press, 2007), 300–18.

BERGER, PETER, GRACE DAVIE, and EFFIE FOKAS. *Religious America, Secular Europe? A Theme and Variations* (Aldershot: Ashgate, 2008).

BERKHOF, HENDRIKUS. *Christian Faith: An Introduction to the Study of the Faith* (Grand Rapids, MI: Eerdmans, 1979).

BOGOLEPOV, ALEXANDER A. 'Legal Position of the Russian Orthodox Church in the Soviet Union', in R. H. Marshall, Jr (ed.), *Aspects of Religion in the Soviet Union 1917–1967* (Chicago: University of Chicago Press, 1971), 193–222.

BOWLBY, JOHN. *Charles Darwin* (London: Pimlico, 1990).

BOYER, PASCAL. *Religion Explained: The Human Instincts that Fashion Gods, Spirits and Ancestors* (London: Vintage, 2002).

BROOKE, JOHN HEDLEY. 'Natural Law in the Natural Sciences: the Origins of Modern Atheism?', *Science and Christian Belief*, 4 (1992), 83–103.

BROOKE, JOHN and GEOFFREY CANTOR. *Reconstructing Nature: The Engagement of Science and Religion* (Edinburgh: T&T Clark, 1998).

BUCKLEY, MICHAEL. *At the Origins of Modern Atheism* (New Haven: Yale University Press, 1987).

BURRELL, DAVID. 'Islam and Christianity', in Ian McFarland et al. (eds.), *Cambridge Dictionary of Theology* (Cambridge: Cambridge University Press, forthcoming).

BUSS, DAVID M. (ed.). *Handbook of Evolutionary Psychology* (Hoboken, NJ: Wiley & Sons, 2005).

BUTTERFIELD, HERBERT. *Christianity and History* (London: Bell, 1949).

CANTWELL SMITH, WILFRED. *The Meaning and End of Religion* (London: SPCK, 1978).

CARROLL, ROBERT P. *Wolf within the Sheepfold: The Bible as a Problem for Christianity* (London: SPCK, 1991).

COLLINS, FRANCIS. *The Language of God: A Scientist Presents Evidence for Belief* (New York: Free Press, 2006).

COLLINS, JOHN. *The Bible After Babel: Historical Criticism in a Postmodern Age* (Grand Rapids, MI: Eerdmans, 2005).

COLLINS, ROBIN. 'Multiverse Hypothesis: A Theistic Perspective', in Bernard Carr (ed.), *Universe or Multiverse* (Cambridge: Cambridge University Press, 2007), 459–80.

CONWAY MORRIS, SIMON. *Life's Solution: Inevitable Humans in a Lonely Universe* (Cambridge: Cambridge University Press, 2003).

COPAN, PAUL and WILLIAM LANE CRAIG. *Creation out of Nothing: A Biblical, Philosophical and Scientific Exploration* (Grand Rapids, MI: Baker, 2004).

CORNWELL, JOHN. *Darwin's Angel* (London: Profile, 2007).

DALY, M. and M. WILSON. *Homicide* (New York: De Gruyter, 1988).

DARWIN, CHARLES. *The Descent of Man* (London: Penguin, 2004).

DAVIE, GRACE *Europe: The Exceptional Case—Parameters of Faith in the Modern World* (London: Darton, Longman & Todd, 2002).

——*Religion in Britain Since 1945: Believing without Belonging* (Oxford: Blackwell, 1994).

DAVIES, PAUL. *The Goldilocks Enigma: Why is the Universe just Right for Life?* (Harmondsworth: Penguin, 2007).

DAVIS, ELLEN F. 'Critical Traditioning: Seeking an Inner Biblical Hermeneutic', in Ellen F. Davis and Richard B. Hays (eds.), *The Art of Reading Scripture* (Grand Rapids, MI: Eerdmans, 2003), 163–80.

DAWKINS, RICHARD. *The God Delusion* (London: Bantam, 2006).

DENNETT, DANIEL C. *Breaking the Spell: Religion as a Natural Phenomenon* (London: Penguin, 2007).

—— *Darwin's Dangerous Idea* (New York: Touchstone, 1995).

DEVINE, TOM. *Scotland's Shame: Bigotry and Sectarianism in Modern Scotland* (Edinburgh: Mainstream, 2000).

DONNER, FRED M. 'The Historical Context', in Jane Dammen McAuliffe (ed.), *The Cambridge Companion to the Qur'an* (Cambridge: Cambridge University Press, 2006), 23–39.

DRACHMAN, A. B. *Atheism in Pagan Antiquity* (London: Gylendal, 1922).

DUNN, JAMES D. G. 'Criteria for a Wise Reading of a Biblical Text', in David F. Ford and Graham Stanton (eds.), *Reading Texts, Seeking Wisdom* (London: SCM, 2003).

DYSON, FREEMAN. *Disturbing the Universe* (New York: Harper & Row, 1979).

EDGELL, PENNY, JOSEPH GERTEIS, and DOUGLAS HARTMANN. 'Atheists as "Other": Moral Boundaries and Cultural Membership in American Society', *American Sociological Review* 71(2) (2006), 211–34.

ELLIS, GEORGE. 'Multiverses: Description, Uniqueness, and Testing', in Bernard Carr (ed.), *Universe or Multiverse* (Cambridge: Cambridge University Press, 2007), 387–410.

ESPOSITO, JOHN. *Unholy War* (Oxford: Oxford University Press, 2002).

FERGUSSON, DAVID. *Church, State and Civil Society* (Cambridge: Cambridge University Press, 2004).

—— *The Cosmos and the Creator* (London: SPCK, 1998).

FISHBANE, MICHAEL. *The Garments of Torah* (Bloomington: Indiana University Press, 1989).

FORD, DAVID. *Christian Wisdom: Desiring God and Learning in Love* (Cambridge: Cambridge University Press, 2007).

FORD, DAVID F. *Shaping Theology: Engagements in a Religious and Secular World* (Oxford: Blackwell, 2007).

FORREST, BARBARA and PAUL GROSS. *Creationism's Trojan Horse: The Wedge of Intelligent Design* (Oxford: Oxford University Press, 2004).

GENTILE, EMILIO. *Politics as Religion* (Princeton, NJ: Princeton University Press, 2006).

GERRISH, BRIAN. *The Old Protestantism and the New* (Edinburgh: T&T Clark, 1982).

GILLIOT, CLAUDE. 'Exegesis of the Qur'ān: Classical and Medieval', in *Encyclopaedia of the Qur'ān*. General Editor: Jane Dammen McAuliffe (Leiden: Brill Online, 2009). www.brillonline.nl/subscriber/entry?entry=q3_COM-00058 (accessed 11 February 2009).

GODDARD, LISA M. D. *An Interrogation of the Selfishness Paradigm in Sociobiology*. University of Chester, unpublished PhD thesis, 2008.

GOULD, STEPHEN JAY. *Rocks of Ages: Science and Religion in the Fullness of Life* (London: Jonathan Cape, 2001).

GRAHAM, GORDON. *Philosophy of the Arts: An Introduction to Aesthetics*, 2nd edition (London: Routledge, 2000).

GRANT, ROBERT. *A Short History of the Interpretation of the Bible* (London: SCM, 1984).

GREGERSEN, NIELS HENRIK. 'Emergence: What is at Stake for Religious Reflection', in Philip Clayton and Paul Davies (eds.), *The Re-Emergence of Emergence: The Emergentist Hypothesis from Science to Religion* (Oxford: Oxford University Press, 2006), 279–302.

HAMILTON, W. D. 'The Genetical Evolution of Social Behaviour', *Journal of Theoretical Biology*, 7 (1964), 1–16, 17–52.

HARE, JOHN. 'Is There an Evolutionary Foundation for Human Morality?', in Philip Clayton and Jeffrey Schloss (eds.), *Evolution and Ethics: Human Morality in Biological and Religious Perspective* (Grand Rapids, MI: Eerdmans, 2004), 187–203.

HARRIS, SAM. *The End of Faith: Religion, Terror, and the Future of Reason* (Norton: New York, 2004).

HAZLETT, IAN. 'Ebbs and Flows of Theology in Glasgow, 1451–1843', in W. I. P. Hazlett (ed.), *Traditions of Theology in Glasgow 1450–1990* (Edinburgh: Scottish Academic Press, 1993), 1–26.

HAZLETT, W. I. P. (ed.). *Traditions of Theology in Glasgow 1450–1990* (Edinburgh: Scottish Academic Press, 1993).

HECTOR, KEVIN. 'Apophaticism in Thomas Aquinas: A Reformulation and Recommendation', *Scottish Journal of Theology*, 60 (2007), 377–93.

HEIDEGGER, MARTIN. 'On the Origin of the Work of Art', in *Basic Writings*, ed. David Farrell Krell, 2nd edition (London: Routledge, 1993), 139–212.

HILL, CHRISTOPHER. 'Tolerance in Seventeenth-Century England: Theory and Practice', in Susan Mendus (ed.), *The Politics of Toleration* (Edinburgh: Edinburgh University Press, 1999), 27–44.

HILLENBRAND, CAROLE. *The Crusades: Islamic Perspectives* (Edinburgh: Edinburgh University Press, 1999).

HITCHENS, CHRISTOPHER. *God Is Not Great: The Case against Religion* (London: Atlantic Books, 2007).

HOLDER, RODNEY D. *God, the Multiverse and Everything* (Aldershot: Ashgate, 2004).

HUME, DAVID. *An Enquiry concerning the Principles of Morals*, ed. L. A. Selby-Bigge (Oxford: Clarendon, 1975).

HUXLEY, THOMAS. *Collected Essays*, vol. v (London: Macmillan, 1894).

HUYSSTEEN, WENTZEL VAN. *Alone in the World? Human Uniqueness in Science and Theology* (Grand Rapids, MI: Eerdmans, 2006).

INGOLD, TIM. 'Epilogue', in Kathleen R. Gibson and Tim Ingold (eds.), *Tools, Language and Cognition in Human Evolution* (Cambridge: Cambridge University Press, 1993), 447–72.

—— 'From the Transmission of Representations to the Education of Attention', in Harvey Whitehouse (ed.), *The Debated Mind: Evolutionary Psychology versus Ethnography* (Oxford: Berg, 2001), 113–54.

JENKINS, PHILIP. *God's Continent: Christianity, Islam and Europe's Religious Crisis* (Oxford: Oxford University Press, 2007).

JOHNSON, PHILIP E. *Darwin on Trial* (Washington, DC: Regnery Gateway, 1991).

JOYCE, RICHARD. *The Evolution of Morality* (Cambridge, MA: MIT Press, 2007).

KALISCH, MUHAMMED. 'A Muslim View of Judaism', in Perry Schmidt-Leukel and Lloyd Ridgeon (eds.), *Islam and Inter-Faith Relations* (London: SCM, 2007), 67–83.

KEMP SMITH, NORMAN. *The Credibility of Divine Existence: The Collected Papers of Norman Kemp Smith*, ed. A. J. D. Porteous, R. D. Maclennan, and G. E. Davie (London: Macmillan, 1967).

KERR, FERGUS. *After Aquinas: Versions of Thomism* (Oxford: Blackwell, 2002).

—— *Immortal Longings: Versions of Transcending Humanity* (London: SPCK, 1997).

KHOSROKHAVAR, FARHAD. *Suicide Bombers: Allah's New Martyrs* (London: Pluto, 2005).

KRAEMER, DAVID. 'Scriptural Interpretation in the Mishnah', in Magne Saebø (ed.), *Hebrew Bible/Old Testament: The History of Its Interpretation*, vol. i (Göttingen: Vandenhoeck & Ruprecht, 1996), 278–84.

KÜNG, HANS. *Islam: Past, Present & Future* (Oxford: One World, 2007).

LAIDLAW, JAMES. 'A Well-Disposed Anthropologist's Problems with the "Cognitive Science of Religion"', in Harvey Whitehouse and James Laidlaw (eds.), *Religion, Anthropology and Cognitive Science* (Durham, NC: Carolina Academic Press, 2007), 211–46.

LEVENSON, JON D. *The Hebrew Bible, the Old Testament, and Historical Criticism* (Philadelphia: Westminster/John Knox Press, 1993).

LIECHTY, JOSEPH and CECILIA CLEGG. *Moving Beyond Sectarianism: Religion, Conflict and Reconciliation in Northern Ireland* (Dublin: Columba Press, 2001).

MACKIE, J. L. *Ethics: Inventing Right and Wrong* (Harmondsworth: Penguin, 1977).

MACKINNON, DONALD. *Borderlands in Theology* (London: Lutterworth, 1968).

MACMURRAY, JOHN. *Persons in Relation* (London: Faber, 1961).

MANSON, NEIL. *God and Design: The Teleological Argument and Modern Science* (London: Routledge, 2003).

MARTIN, DAVID. *Does Christianity Cause War?* (Oxford: Oxford University Press, 1997).

MARTIN, LUTHER H. 'Religion and Cognition', in John Hinnells (ed.), *Routledge Companion to the Study of Religion* (London: Routledge, 2005), 473–88.

McCABE, HERBERT. *God Matters* (London: Chapman, 1987).

McEWAN, IAN. *Saturday* (London: Vintage, 2006).

McGRATH, ALISTER. *Dawkins' God: Genes, Memes and the Meaning of Life* (Oxford: Blackwell, 2005).

McGRATH, ALISTER with JOANNA COLLICUT. *The Dawkins Delusion? Atheist Fundamentalism and the Denial of the Divine* (London: SPCK, 2007).

McMULLIN, ERNEST. 'Cosmic Purpose and the Contingency of Human Evolution', *Theology Today*, 55 (1998/99), 389–414.

McTERNAN, OLIVER. *Violence in God's Name: Religion in an Age of Conflict* (London: Darton, Longman & Todd, 2003).

MIDDLETON, PAUL. *Radical Martyrdom and Cosmic Conflict in Early Christianity* (London: T&T Clark, 2006).

MILL, JOHN STUART. *Collected Works*, vol. 1 (Toronto: Toronto University Press, 1981).

MILLER, KENNETH. *Finding Darwin's God: A Scientist's Search for Common Ground between God and Evolution* (Harper: New York, 1999).

MOJZES, PAUL. *Religion and the War in Bosnia* (Atlanta: Scholars Press, 1998).

MOSSNER, ERNEST. *The Life of David Hume*, 2nd edition (Oxford: Oxford University Press, 1980).

MURDOCH, IRIS. *The Fire and the Sun* (Oxford: Oxford University Press, 1977).

——*Sartre: Romantic Rationalist* (London: Collins, 1967).

NEUWIRTH, ANGELIKA. 'Qur'an and History—a Disputed Relationship: Some Reflections of Qur'anic History and History in the Qur'an', *Journal of Qur'anic Studies*, 5 (2003), 1–18.

NEWMAN, JOHN HENRY. *University Sermons* (London: SPCK, 1970).

NIEZTSCHE, FRIEDRICH. *The Gay Science*, ed. Bernard Williams (Cambridge: Cambridge University Press, 2001).

NOLL, MARK. *The Civil War as a Theological Crisis* (Durham, NC: University of North Carolina Press, 2006).

NORRIS, PIPPA and RONALD INGLEHARDT. *Sacred and Secular: Religion and Politics Worldwide* (Cambridge: Cambridge University Press, 2004).

OCKER, C. 'Biblical Interpretation in the Middle Ages', in Donald McKim (ed.), *Dictionary of Major Biblical Interpreters* (Downers' Grove, IL: IVP 2007), 14–21.

O'SHEA, STEPHEN. *Sea of Faith: Islam and Christianity in the Medieval Mediterranean World* (London Profile, 2006).

PAUL, DIANE B. 'Darwin, Social Darwinism and Eugenics', in Jonathan Hodge (ed.), *The Cambridge Companion to Darwin* (Cambridge: Cambridge University Press, 2003), 214–39.

PEIRCE, CHARLES SANDERS. *Collected Papers*, vol. VI: *Scientific Metaphysics* (Cambridge, MA: Harvard University Press, 1935).

PHIPPS, WILLIAM E. *Darwin's Religious Odyssey* (Harrisburg, PA: Trinity Press International, 2002).

PINKER, STEPHEN. *How the Mind Works* (London: Penguin, 1998).

PLANTINGA, ALVIN. 'Religion and Epistemology', in Edward Craig (ed.), *Routledge Encyclopedia of Philosophy* (London: Routledge, 1998), vol. VIII: 209–17.

——*Warrant and Proper Function* (New York: Oxford University Press, 1993).

PUTNAM, HILARY. *Meaning and the Moral Sciences* (London: Routledge & Kegan Paul, 1978).

RALSTON, HOLMES, III. 'Inevitable Humans: Simon Conway Morris's Evolutionary Paleontology', *Zygon*, 40 (2005), 221–9.

RAMADAN, TARIQ. *Western Muslims and the Future of Islam* (Oxford: Oxford University Press, 2004).

REES, MARTIN. *Just Six Numbers: The Deep Forces that Shape the Universe* (London: Weidenfeld & Nicolson, 1999).

—— 'Other Universes: A Scientific Perspective', in Neil Manson (ed.). *God and Design: The Teleological Argument and Modern Science* (London: Routledge, 2003), 211–20.

REID, H. B. M. *The Divinity Professors in the University of Glasgow* (Glasgow, 1923).

REIF, STEFAN C. 'Aspects of the Jewish Contribution to Biblical Interpretation', in John Barton (ed.), *Cambridge Companion to Biblical Interpretation* (Cambridge: Cambridge University Press, 1998), 143–59.

RILEY-SMITH, JONATHAN. 'Rethinking the Crusades', *First Things* (March 2000), 20–3.

—— *What Were the Crusades?*, 3rd edition (London: Palgrave Macmillan, 2002).

RUSE, MICHAEL. *Taking Darwin Seriously* (Oxford: Blackwell, 1986).

RUSSELL, BERTRAND. *A Free Man's Worship* (London: Unwin, 1976).

—— *Why I Am Not a Christian* (London: Unwin, 1957).

SARTRE, JEAN-PAUL. *Existentialism and Humanism* (London: Methuen, 1948).

SMITH, ADAM. *An Inquiry into the Nature and Causes of The Wealth of Nations* (Oxford: Clarendon, 1976).

—— *Lectures on Jurisprudence* (Oxford: Clarendon, 1978).

STEWART, M. A. 'Rational Religion and Common Sense', in Joseph Houston (ed.), *Thomas Reid: Context, Influence and Significance* (Edinburgh: Dunedin Academic Press, 2004), 123–60.

—— 'Religion and Rational Theology', in Alexander Broadie (ed.), *The Cambridge Companion to the Scottish Enlightenment* (Cambridge: Cambridge University Press, 2003), 31–59.

STOUT, JEFFREY. *Ethics After Babel* (Cambridge: Clarke, 1988).

SUTHERLAND, STEWART R. *Atheism and the Rejection of God: Contemporary Philosophy and the Brothers Karamazov* (Oxford: Blackwell, 1977).

SWINBURNE, RICHARD. *The Existence of God* (Oxford: Clarendon Press, 1979).

TAYLOR, CHARLES. *A Secular Age* (Cambridge, MA: Harvard University Press, 2007).

THOMAS, R. S. *Collected Later Poems 1998–2000* (Tarset: Bloodaxe Books, 2004).

THROWER, JAMES. *Western Atheism: A Short History* (New York: Prometheus Books, 2000).

TIL, HOWARD VAN. 'The Creation: Intelligently Designed or Optimally Equipped?', *Theology Today*, 55 (1998/9), 344–64.

TOBIN, MAUREEN and ROBIN TOBIN (eds.). *How Long O Lord? Christian, Jewish and Muslim Voices from the Ground and Visions for the Future* (Cambridge, MA: Cowley, 2002).

UPDIKE, JOHN. *Villages* (London: Penguin, 2006).

WAAL, FRANS DE. *Primates and Philosophers: How Morality Evolved*, ed. Stephen Macedo and Josiah Ober (Princeton, NJ: Princeton University Press, 2006).

WAINES, DAVID. *An Introduction to Islam*, 2nd edition (Cambridge: Cambridge University Press, 2003).

WANSBROUGH, JOHN. *Quranic Studies: Sources and Methods of Scriptural Interpretation* (Oxford: Oxford University Press, 1977).

WARD, KEITH. *Is Religion Dangerous?* (London: Lion Hudson, 2006).

WIGNER, EUGENE. 'The Unreasonable Effectiveness of Mathematics in the Natural Sciences', *Communications in Pure and Applied Mathematics*, 13.1 (1960), 1–14.

WILSON, A. N. *God's Funeral* (London: John Murray, 1999).

WILSON, DAVID SLOAN. *Darwin's Cathedral: Evolution, Religion and the Nature of Society* (Chicago: University of Chicago Press, 2002).

WILSON, EDWARD O. and MICHAEL RUSE. 'Moral Philosophy as Applied Science', *Philosophy*, 61 (1986), 173–92.

WITTGENSTEIN, LUDWIG. *Lectures and Conversations on Aesthetics, Psychology and Religious Belief* (Oxford: Blackwell, 1966).

WOOTTON, DAVID. 'New Histories of Atheism', in Michael Hunter and David Wooton (eds.), *Atheism from the Reformation to the Enlightenment* (Oxford: Oxford University Press, 1992), 13–54.

ZUCKERMAN, PHIL. 'Atheism: Contemporary Numbers and Patterns', in Michael Martin (ed.), *Cambridge Companion to Atheism* (Cambridge: Cambridge University Press, 2004), 47–65.

INDEX

Scripture Index

Qur'an Index

Pre–Modern References

Subject Index